To Kathryn

With best wishes.

George Ward.

FORT GRUNWICK

George Ward

FORT GRUNWICK

Temple Smith · London

First Published in Great Britain 1977
By Maurice Temple Smith Ltd
37 Great Russell Street, London WC1

Second impression 1978

© 1977 George Ward
ISBN 0 85117 146X Cased
ISBN 0 85117 1478 Paperback

Film set and printed by
Billing & Sons Limited
Guildford, Worcester & London

Contents

FORT GRUNWICK

1

Why I fight

Fort Grunwick? Well, that is what it has felt like. For more than a year, our photo-finishing company in north-west London has been subjected to a state of siege. I have written this book because I would like people to understand what the experience is like; why all of us at Grunwick have persisted in taking a stand that some may feel to be unreasonable or obdurate; and why we believe that what is at stake is not just the future of one small company but a vital matter of principle that deeply concerns us all.

One thing must be said straightaway. I did not pick a fight and I do not want to continue fighting for a moment longer than necessary. Our opponents have said more than once that they want to wipe our business out: on my side I do not want to wipe *them* out. I have no wish to end trade unionism in Britain. It has been in the past, and could again be in the future, an important force for good. I oppose what I see as the misuse of a great tradition for ignoble ends, the tyranny of an apparatus that has become more concerned with perpetuating and increasing its own power than with the welfare of the workers it claims to represent.

The pickets have said that they are besieging Grunwick because we will not permit our workers to join a trade union. This is a complete fabrication, as has been proved in the hearings of successive industrial tribunals, and in the Scarman court of inquiry. I have never dismissed an employee for joining a union, and there are a number of union members still working for the company. But this is different from granting an official status to the union by 'recognition', giving it the contractual right to negotiate with the company. In practice this means that the union is likely to seek to negotiate not just for its own members but for the whole workforce, and eventually it may try to impose a closed shop, excluding from employment all those who refuse to join. We are not prepared to accept that our company should be compelled to recognise a union to which the overwhelming majority of our workers have no wish to belong, and *which could not boast a single member at Grunwick (or in the entire photo-finishing industry) at the time it chose to intervene in a minor dispute.*

Nor are we prepared to accept the unions' other major demand: that we should reinstate strikers who were lawfully dismissed for breach of contract and industrial misconduct—which included, on the part of some of them, violent rioting and the destruction of property. Nor are we prepared to let Grunwick move one inch in the direction of the closed shop, that ultimate affront to liberty. The union that wants to get into Grunwick says it would not insist on the closed shop, but it has imposed the closed shop at other companies in the past, and I prefer to judge by deeds, not words.

Because we have chosen to be guided by the laws of England and by the wishes of our workers, we have been called more hard names than I care to recall—or my publisher might care to print. One of the delegates at the 1977 conference of the Trades Union Congress in Blackpool got up and dubbed me a 'rogue elephant'. You don't argue with such beasts, he went on; you try to stop them in their tracks. That was relatively mild stuff. Mick McGahey, the Communist boss of the Scottish miners, has called me an 'industrial hooligan'. The *Daily Mirror* claimed I was running 'a slave labour factory'. Laurie Pavitt, a left-wing Labour MP, told the House of Commons that I ran a Dickensian 'sweat-shop'. The 'moderate' Roy Grantham, leader of the white-collar workers' union, the Association of Professional, Executive, Clerical and Computer Staff, APEX, (which set the whole thing in motion by trying to impose itself on our company) tagged me 'a reactionary employer' and an 'inflexible, hard-line anti-trade unionist'.

I have grown fairly thick-skinned about all of this. I don't much care what people think of me; I care what *I* think of me. What surprises me more than the insults is the claim by many union spokesmen that the stand we have taken at Grunwick poses a threat to trade unionism in Britian. Some of their statements suggest that they regard the battle at Grunwick as a test of their virility, and that their fear of losing is as intense and as visceral as some men's fear of impotence. Chris Wright, another senior APEX man has declared that 'if we lose this one, we will lose them all'. Tom Jackson, the cuddly, bewhiskered chief of the Union of Post Office Workers, has said that 'if we can't crack Grunwick, we can't crack anything.'

Yet at the root of all this is a small company that employed fewer than five hundred people at the beginning of the dispute, and now employs only about half that number. Hardly a daunting target for the combined forces of the TUC, which represents 11.6 million unionised workers and has been backed by the Labour government and by every organised left-wing group in the country.

In their efforts to force Grunwick to recognise a union to which our workers have demonstrated they have no wish to belong, these big battalions have used all the weapons of industrial warfare. They have beseiged the company with thousands of menacing pickets. They have harassed our workers in their own homes, abused and assaulted them in the streets and cinemas, painted abusive words on their doors and even threatened to kidnap one girl's three-year-old child. They have tried to cut off our supplies. They have persuaded union members at Heathrow airport to refuse to handle our foreign trade. They have picketed and harangued the chemists who send film to us for developing. They have illegally blacked our mail. They have threatened to cut off our water, gas and electricity, to deny us the services of the fire brigade in the event of arson or accidental fire, and to freeze our bank accounts.

On top of all the violence and intimidation, we have also had to contend with political pressure from the government; and we have been saddened by the lack of support from some people in other parties on whose concern for individual liberty we thought we could depend.

Somehow, we have managed to survive. I suppose this explains the near-hysteria with which union 'moderates', as well as Marxist extremists, discuss Grunwick. The company has not only been 'unreasonable' enough to insist that it will act in accordance with the law and the wishes of its workers, whether or not this suits the unions; it has held out. In the words of the French proverb, 'This animal is very wicked; when attacked, it defends itself.'

My sole concern has always been to maintain a successful small business that provides jobs for our workers and an efficient service to the public. I had no wish to see that business become a battlefield where unions could demonstrate their invincible might and bring other 'recalcitrant' companies or non-unionised workers to heel. I do not believe it is an exaggeration to say that they wanted to demonstrate that it is only possible to pursue a business or get a job in England today on their terms. They assumed that, since they had succeeded in imposing their terms on many bigger companies in the past, it would take no great effort to bring a relatively small company to heel. Grunwick has disappointed them.

We have fought for our rights and for those of our workers under the law because we are hostile to all forms of tyranny. We would rather close down the business and pay compensation to our workers than agree to conduct it on the terms of organised bullies. I think it is fair to say that if bigger employers had taken this line in the past, Britain would not be as close to the corporate state—in other words, left-wing Fascism—as it is.

I have never been opposed to trade unionism in principle, and I have never denied our workers the right to join a union if they wish. What I have always opposed is the desire of unions to coerce people to join a union against their will. The very fact that my attitude is represented as reactionary is a symptom of how far Britain has declined towards a kind of society in which the individual will have no rights unless he is a member of the right corporate body.

Win or lose, the resistance that has been put up by Fort Grunwick will have been more than worthwhile if two lessons are drawn from it by the community at large. The first is that misused trade union power is not invincible, that it must be brought within civilised bounds, and that no one who has any respect for freedom can deny that along with a worker's right to join a union goes his right *not* to join, if he so chooses. The second is that, however necessary trade unions may have been in the past, and however good the purposes they can still serve, they have recently exposed their unacceptable face. Jack Dromey, the local strike organiser, talked fervently about the 'sacred rights' of the unions. I doubt whether, after Grunwick, any sizeable proportion of the British public will be inclined to agree that the union official is the closest man to God. A Gallup poll published in September 1977 showed that 75 per cent of the British think that the unions have too much power.

Other union spokesmen have called me a nineteenth-century employer. In truth, it is the mentality of the union leaders that belongs to the last century. The leadership of Britain's trade union movement today constitutes an arrogant and reactionary establishment. Like any establishment, it produces myths to justify its privileges, claiming that it stands for workers' solidarity and the 'sacred right' of collective bargaining when what it wants is more power. Grunwick has already become part of the union mythology, to be recorded in the annals along with the Tolpuddle Martyrs or the Peterloo Massacre. But this time, the unions do not represent the underdog.

The battle at Grunwick has never been a fight between an employer and the workers. Management and staff at Grunwick have been united in opposing the unions' demands. One of the newspaper cartoons depicted me standing on a pedestal with arms folded, while a hail of missiles is flung at me from below. The image of the lone fighter is flattering, but profoundly misleading. My battle could never have been fought without the loyalty and quiet courage of workers and friends inside the company, many of whom feel as strongly as I do about the issues of principle that have been at stake, and many of whom have been exposed to tremendous pressure.

I think, for example, of Azadi Patel. Azadi is a young mother (she was twenty-eight when the dispute began) who came to England from Uganda in 1967. She started work in the mail order department in the spring of 1975. Through the weeks of the mass pickets, Azadi would get up at six every morning to cook her husband's lunch, and then take her three-year-old son to the child-minder before going to the pick-up point to catch the company bus at 7.20 a.m. She has always turned up for work, even on the day the unions had threatened to bring 25,000 pickets down to beat the company to its knees.

Azadi had to put up with continual harassment from the pickets. She received threatening phone calls. Anonymous callers told her they would 'get her' if she refused to join the strike. They even threatened to kidnap her three-year-old baby. One night, someone painted the word 'Scab' in big white letters on her green front door. At the end of May 1977 she was taking her son to the child-minder when some of the pickets went by in a minibus. They slowed down and started screaming abuse at her. Some of them threw gravel at her, without any concern for the safety of her child, and then drove off laughing. She stopped going to the cinema after some of her friends were abused by people who sat in the row behind them, muttering insults.

Azadi did not let any of this frighten her. She is one of the many workers at Grunwick who have said repeatedly that they would leave if the strikers were reinstated and they were forced to work with the people who had threatened and abused them.

I think of Hilda Watte, who works in the colour processing department at Cobbold Road. Hilda has plenty of experience of fighting tyranny. Her family came to East Germany as refugees from Russia. When she left school after the war, aged fifteen, she was told that she would not be able to get a job unless she joined the Communist youth movement. Instead she ran away from home and spent three days and nights smuggling herself over the border into West Germany. Hilda has no love of Communists, and does not like being pushed around. She says, 'I wouldn't knuckle down to the Communist Youth to get a job. Why should I have to knuckle down to a shop steward? Doesn't it amount to the same thing?'

I think of Comfort Candy, another fighter, a handsome Ashanti girl from Ghana. She won't let anyone tell her how to run her life. She's always nicely turned out, and has her own flat in Kilburn. At the start of the trouble, the pickets were shouting at her, 'Such a lovely girl—where do you think you're going?' She tells them off in no uncertain terms. 'It's a free country,' she says, 'if they want to, they can hang about outside, but I love working at Grunwick and I've got every right to work where I like. If I didn't like it, I'd have walked out long ago.'

The courage of the girls of Grunwick—and of the young executives who have turned themselves into volunteer bus-drivers or come in each morning at the crack of dawn to ensure we beat the pickets—is what has kept us going. Also we have found many friends outside, and the postbag has brought daily evidence of the depth of feeling the conflict has aroused up and down the country.

I need quote only one letter. It comes from a resident of Cooper Road, which runs behind our Chapter Road factory—one of the many local residents who for months had to put up with mobs of howling pickets trampling over their front gardens. It might have been understandable if someone in his position had blamed us for the disruption of his daily life. But he wrote, on 26 August, 1977:

May I, as a resident of Cooper Road, assure you that I believe that the vast majority of people support you in your stand and ask you please to consider that residents such as myself have had to put up with scenes and damage reminiscent of Northern Ireland in front of our homes. If

you give the concessions which appear to be expected of
you by the newspaper reports I would feel that the
discomfort and inconvenience we have suffered would have
been in vain. I realise that pressure must be being put upon
you from all sides, but would assure you that a lot of
people still support you.

We received similar letters from postmasters, trade union
members, retired brigadiers, old age pensioners, small
businessmen, Asian shopkeepers, students, university
professors and even the occasional City chairman. They all
strengthened my conviction that Fort Grunwick will stand,
and that its stand may even be remembered as a turning-
point in Britain's social history: as a point at which public
opinion revolted against the destruction of civil rights by
unrepresentative union leaders whose behaviour is a betrayal
of the original ideals of the trade union movement, and began
to demand corrective action.

Britain has never tolerated bullies for long. I hope that our
stand at Grunwick will hasten the day when the union tyrant
with a licence to conscript labour will vanish into the museum
of social history, like the feudal landlord and the Dickensian
employer before him.

2

I chose England

I am not a native-born Briton but an immigrant Anglo-Indian, the descendant of a merchant adventurer from Norwich who went out to Bombay to seek his fortune in the latter part of the last century. Perhaps this is why I cling so fiercely to the values and traditions that made Britain great and why I am so disappointed to find that, as Britain's power and self-confidence have declined, so has the respect for freedom under law.

I was born in New Delhi in 1933, the youngest son of two Anglo-Indians. My father was a successful accountant and for the first few years of my life the family lived very comfortably. In 1938 the crash came. He lost a great deal of money in a series of unwise investments, our fortunes plummeted and he himself came close to a nervous breakdown. My mother, a loyal and determined woman, took charge. She decided to pack the whole family off to England for an extended vacation.

My grandmother was living in Greenwich and my parents identified as closely with England as with India, and were probably more devoted to it, like many Anglo-Indians. But the England of 1938 was an England in turmoil and confusion. While my parents were house-hunting in Kent, Chamberlain was setting off for Munich. While the papers editorialised about peace in our time, we were all being issued with gas masks and contingency plans were being drawn up to ship children off to Canada. My father, then fifty-three and in bad health, was convinced that war would come and concerned that it might separate him from his children.

What the threat of war meant to me, aged five, was a visit to be fitted for a gas mask, resembling a pig's snout. Its possible uses were then incomprehensible to me. Convinced that it was designed to protect me from bombs as well as gas I put its usefulness to the test by delivering a swift clip over the ear to my aunt who was with me for the same purpose. She was the kind of woman who hits back; her forceful response made me instantly aware that a gas mask is no protection against a bomb.

In October 1938, just after Munich, we set sail for Bombay on the SS Britannia. When we got back to India nobody could understand me because I was already a thorough Cockney. In 1940 I was packed off to a boarding school in Darjeeling called Mount Hermon, which was run by American Methodist missionaries.

I had had a pact with my father that if I found life at boarding school intolerable, he would get me out of it just as soon as I sent him a coded message. This was to take the form of a picture of a duck with some eggs which I was to send to him at the required moment. When I got bored and homesick, I duly drew up this coded message and sent it off. To my shock and disillusionment, my father did not leap to the rescue. Instead, he took me up to the same school the following year. This, as it turned out, was the last time I saw him. He died of a cerebral haemorrhage in 1941.

What followed were dark times for the family. Our style of living changed abruptly. My father died intestate with his financial affairs in a total mess. My mother had to give up our apartment and sell most of the contents. We moved into a cramped little flat in a tenement called Jankee Mansions, that amounted to one room and a kitchen. My mother was forced to go to work as a shorthand typist at the railway company where my father had been the deputy chief auditor. Her salary was a pittance, and out of it she had to look after myself and my sister, Georgena.

The events that followed my father's death showed that he had been wrong about one thing; you could not escape the war by going from England to India. Japanese armies were on the borders of India at Assam. They had street-bombed Rangoon, and there were reports of an imminent attack on Calcutta itself. Early in 1942 Georgena and I were evacuated up country to a dusty, hot little town called Gorakhpur. The local officials, in the best British tradition, exercised themselves in ordering local residents to dig trenches in their front gardens. The trenches completely vanished from view during the monsoon.

When the immediate threat of an attack on Calcutta receded, we returned to the city. My mother could no longer afford to send me to Mount Hermon, so I was sent instead to the local Jesuit college. I suffered there for a period under a particularly unpleasant teacher whose speciality was rapping boys across the knuckles with a heavy ruler. I escaped in 1943, when my mother scraped together enough money to send me to a boarding school run by the Irish Christian Brothers at Kurseong, in the Himalayan foothills near Darjeeling. This is a region of towering pine forests and arching mountain ranges, of deep gorges and waterfalls where women come to wash their clothes, and villagers to burn their dead. I would be sent up to the school every year in March for a solid period of nine months, travelling up on the mail train from Sealdah in Calcutta, to the last railway station of the plains, Siliguri, where I would have to change to the Darjeeling-Himalayan Railway, nicknamed the 'Dirty, Hard-up Railway' by the schoolboys. Despite the discomforts of the train, a thrill would go through me in the black night at the sight of rolling fields of fireflies, glimmering in the dark, as if the Milky Way had been spread out at my feet. As the dawn broke over those vast plains, the sun looked like a red ball rolling along the horizon beside the train.

At Kurseong, I was made to go to Mass every day, which failed to make me a real Catholic: that came later. Our study periods took place every evening under the drab, intermittent light from the school's own dynamo, which harnessed the power of the waterfall above the school. The Christian Brothers were stern task-masters; they demanded high standards, and generally got them. The most lasting impression on me was left by a brilliant teacher of Portuguese origin called Orie Gomez, now known as Brother Peter. The school motto was 'Omnia bene facere', 'Do all things well'. It stuck with me.

It was in 1948, after independence, that my mother decided to take me to England for the second time. She believed there would be no future in the new India for Anglo-Indians like ourselves, who were condemned to be treated as the children of the Raj. We had been living in Calcutta during the bloody race riots between Hindus and Muslims, and she feared that the Anglo-Indian community itself might be the target of future racial disturbances. About this time the father of one of my school friends, the manager of a jute mill not far from Calcutta and an Anglo-Indian like ourselves, was set upon and hacked to pieces. With the British Army pulling out, no one in our position could be sure that anyone would defend him in the event of an emergency.

It was not easy to get a passage back to England. In the end my mother managed to find us room on a former troop ship that had been converted for passenger use. Our cabin was down below the water line, with no portholes, and it was like a furnace for most of the voyage. Many nights we went upstairs to sleep on deck rather than suffer the heat. We docked at Liverpool towards the end of October 1948 and went down by train to Euston. Second impressions of England, the England I could scarcely remember from before, were not entirely favourable: the drab streets and overcast skies of Liverpool, after the sun and warmth of India; the toy villages after the majestic panoramas of the Himalayan foothills. My mother had arrived with just twelve pounds ten shillings in her handbag.

As a fifteen-year-old immigrant, one thing was plain to me at once. I had to get a job, and as quickly as possible. My first employment in England was as postboy to a wholesale clothiers' firm, Bartram Harvey, near Piccadilly. They paid me precisely two pounds ten shillings a week. Two years was enough to teach me that I was getting nowhere fast. If I was going to make any progress I would have to study for it.

We were living in a bedsitter in Porchester Square in Bayswater, with a gas meter and communal bath. But we

were able to get ourselves into a council flat in Maitland Park
in 1950. Revisiting the flat, I find it poky and wonder that
the rooms seemed airy, even opulent, to me at the time. It
was just that we had had to accustom ourselves to poverty;
even a council flat seemed like the Ritz.

Anxious to get ahead, I put my name down for the Regent
Street Polytechnic. While waiting to hear whether they could
admit me, I got myself a temporary job working for a
watchmaker above a jeweller's shop in Praed Street. He
vanished under mysterious circumstances, with Special
Branch hot on his tail, leaving me with a taste for smoked
salmon—which was his consuming obsession—and my first
whiff of political intrigue. I got into the Regent Street Poly
and won my matriculation in six months. The Principal there
was sufficiently impressed with me to get me a scholarship to
study economics.

I toyed with the idea of becoming an economist, but
dropped it as soon as I learned that there are precious few
jobs going for people with economics degrees who want to
make a career out of them. I had no time for intellectual
luxuries. Accountancy seemed to be the practical thing.
There was an additional spur: my mother had always wanted
me to be an accountant like my father. The snag was that it
was by no means easy for someone born and raised in India,
and of a distinctly dusky hue, to get articles.

I had an unpleasant taste of racial discrimination when I
pursued my luck in interviews with one or two small accountancy firms that had no doubt imagined, from my name, that
I was purely English. I got an immediate rebuff when they
saw the colour of my skin. After this, I took the precaution of
mentioning my origins in letters of application. My lucky
break came after two months of hunting in 1952, when I
visited a firm of accountants in Kings Cross called Burke,
Covington and Nash. I was offered articles, and the princely
sum of one pound a week, and I considered myself a lucky
man. After I joined the firm, I discovered that my national
insurance stamp was deducted from my pound a week.

To finance my studies, my mother worked during the day

as a typist at India House and spent her evenings serving at Lyons Corner House at Marble Arch. She rarely got home before midnight. My sister Georgena was working as a punch operator at the Hudson's Bay Company. Between them, my mother and sister were making it possible for me to get ahead. I took my studies far more seriously than most of the young men I knew at that time, since I knew that my family's hopes were vested in me. After getting home from the office in the evening, I would study from six until ten or eleven at night through a correspondence course. Unfortunately I overworked and eventually burned myself out, to the extent that I had to take a break from evening studies for about eighteen months in order to recover from nervous exhaustion.

I had to make constant mental adjustments in response to the racial attitudes of that time. I ran across firms that refused to allow anyone other than an Englishman born and bred to do their audits. Luckily for me, Burke, Covington and Nash tried not to expose me to this kind of embarrassment. When it did occur, they would insist that it was up to them, not their clients, to choose the accountants to deal with particular jobs.

When I finally qualified as an accountant in 1959, I decided I must leave the firm. I had been reasonably happy at Burke, Covington and Nash, but needed more experience. I moved to a bigger firm which employed some four hundred people. Things did not work out well there. It was partly my fault: I spent too much time and energy trying to catch up on my social life after years of solid swotting. I also collided with a partner who seemed to me to be particularly severe. I saw a way out when I caught sight of an advertisement for a job in Brazil. Deloitte, Plender, Griffiths & Company wanted an accountant for a three-year contract in Rio.

I landed the job and had few qualms about leaving England at this stage. My life had been fairly drab and for obvious reasons England was associated in my mind with hardship, discomforts and racial discrimination, and with the lack of opportunity to get ahead. I was still ensnared in a sort of underdog complex. It partly stemmed from the fact that I am an Anglo-Indian. At the time I left England for Brazil I was still very lacking in self-confidence. I had started out with few assets: I am not very tall and, I am sorry to say, I regard myself as neither handsome nor brilliant, while my family had no money or social status to offer me in Britain. I had not had any real chance to prove myself.

Before I left England, I was over-conscious of the colour difference. There were very few coloured immigrants to be seen in London in those days—not that greater numbers were to lessen the friction! This sometimes used to make me very depressed and often made me feel inhibited living in London. In a more personal sense, I felt that I had missed out altogether on being a normal teenager or a normal young man about town, because of lack of money and the sheer necessity of keeping my nose to the grindstone. My mother and sister had both done a tremendous amount for me, but their dominant influence may have served to stifle my personality.

So I felt *different.* I was also coming to feel that the people around me were living in a kind of society that dampened down individual initiative, a society that was running out of dynamism. I had not reached any conclusions about why this was happening to Britain. But Brazil, from afar, seemed by contrast a country of almost limitless new horizons; President Juscelino Kubitschek had just built Brazilia, that fantastic city in the shape of an aeroplane.

One of the reasons that I chose Brazil was that it had a long history as an independent country. I also had a romantic image of it, and I could see myself beside the waving palm trees. I longed to get back to the tropics. I needed the sunshine again, I needed something that I had not been able to find in England. I had a serious intent as well: I wanted to see whether I could stand on my own two feet as an accountant.

From the outset I was moving on a more exalted plane than I had known before. I was dealing with big companies preparing complete audits. One initial difficulty was that I arrived with no knowledge of Portuguese. But it is never a bad thing to be thrown in at the deep end. Within a year I had mastered the language. I was amused by the response of the Brazilians I dealt with. In appearance, of course, I could pass for a Rio or Sao Paulo businessman. When I arrived, some of my Brazilian friends would say that I was 'the Brazilian Englishman'. By the time I left, they had concluded that I was more English than the English themselves.

I did not lead the free-wheeling life for which Rio is justly celebrated. I was deeply concerned with my religion at that time, and went to Mass every day. I did a great deal of reading, especially history and poetry.

As an outsider, I was hardly aware of the tremendous political changes that were taking place in Brazil in the three years I was there. The turmoil that the country experienced under Janio Quadros and then Joao Goulart had a comic-opera appearance to an outsider, although I could grasp that the failure to control inflation was the critical reason for the political crisis that finally led to a military coup. I was insulated to a large extent, within the foreign business community, from Brazil's own political upheavals.

What impressed me more was the free market situation in which Brazilian industry had been able to develop and expand. In Brazil, if you were a goer, you went. While the British unions were talking about the length of their teabreaks and relativities, Brazil was inventing whole new industries overnight—a car industry, a chemical industry, a clothing industry, an electronics industry. The Brazilians were finding new lands to conquer within their own frontiers, opening up vast swathes of the interior, throwing highways into areas that had never been properly explored.

Brazil enabled me to prove to myself that I could compete with an international set, and that neither my background nor my colour would be obstacles to me in any project if I were ready to give enough of myself to it. Brazilian society sloughed off many of the inhibitions from which I had suffered in England. When I returned to Britain, I was no longer the baby brother; I had grown up.

I came back to England in the summer of 1963, via

Trinidad and New York. My original three-year contract at Deloittes had expired, but I went back to London with a return ticket to Rio in my pocket, convinced that this would only be a holiday. It turned out differently. What happened to me in the months after I returned to London set me on the course I have been pursuing ever since. I cannot say that I understood at this moment the real sources of Britain's disease, or how they would come to affect me, or that I would ever be cast in anything like the role I was later to assume. What I did find encouraging in 1963 was that conditions for business in Britain were more favourable than before. I was also less conscious of the racial difference, after my three years in multi-racial, free-wheeling Brazil.

But it was the combined influence of new friends and the accountancy firm where I had started my career that produced the strongest inducements to forget about my return ticket to Rio. I went round to see Burke, Covington and Nash and found that they were badly in need of extra help. They offered me a partnership, and I took it.

England to a newcomer is rather like a good wine. It takes experience, if not training, to learn fully to savour the bouquet, the depth, the body. The strength and the tradition of this great country is something that is either born with you or must be slowly absorbed. And such things are most easily grasped, I suppose, through the quality of individual people. Those that I met after my return from Rio, and others who have become my closest friends since, convinced me that Britain is not only the most pleasant country in the world to live in but that it can achieve anything—so long as those entrusted with its fortunes have the will and the courage to meet the challenge of their times.

I was living as before, with my mother and sister in the flat at Maitland Park. I was still strongly preoccupied by religion, and was attending Mass regularly at St Dominic's Priory in Southampton Road. It was there that I met my future wife, Loretto. It was there also that I met John Hickey and Tony Grundy, the two men with whom I laid plans for starting a new business which we came to call Grunwick. The name is an acronym of our three surnames; I contented myself with the 'W' in the middle, which is not pronounced by most Oxbridge newscasters. None of us had any inkling that 'Grunwick' was to become, as *Tass* and *Pravda* later declared, a household word throughout the world.

3

Success in the making

The idea of Grunwick was born on one of the long Sunday walks that John Hickey and I used to take across Hampstead Heath after attending Mass at St Dominic's. At that time John was working for a Swedish business equipment firm, but he had experience of photo-finishing when he worked for Cooper & Pearson, an old family firm that later merged with Grunwick. Over a lunchtime drink at one of the pubs on the other side of the Heath, John told me that we could set up a photographic laboratory for £75. So we proceeded to rent a garage in St John's Wood that I saw advertised in a local paper.

We opened the business in Loudoun Road Mews at the beginning of March 1965, at the end of a long winter when the snow was still on the ground. Our understanding was that John would look after production, Tony Grundy would run around drumming up business, and I would keep my partnership in the City while doing the books. We had no staff, and next to no money—which was a real problem since John's estimated budget turned out to be more than a little optimistic. We had spent almost £1,000 before the laboratory was actually opened, and most of it came from me, since I was the chap with the most money at that stage. I sold my open return ticket to Brazil to raise extra cash.

These were the days when Grunwick really was a sweatshop—for the three partners. When he first set eyes on the premises, Tony said 'I don't mind starting from nothing, but this is minus nothing'. We had to put the telephone on the floor,as we had no table for it.

I would come into the company most days after work and every weekend to help with the processing. At the outset, we had to do everything by hand, and dipping the strips of photographic prints into one trough after another made me feel that I was working in a Chinese laundry. John Hickey would start work at eight o'clock in the morning and work until literally any time at night—sometimes right around the clock—while paying himself a gross £10 a week. Tony would run around town looking for new retail outlets all morning, and come in to help with the processing in the afternoon. It was a vicious circle for him: the more orders he was able to get, the more work he would have to do in the afternoon and evening.

I sank my life savings into the company, and worked until two most nights. I saw no return for my investment in the first two years. But little by little, by offering better terms and quicker delivery than our competitors, we managed to get ahead, and brought in my sister Jean and Mary, John's fiancée, to help from time to time. I suppose that what drove all of us on was the feeling that you may only have one big opportunity to get ahead in life, and that you will only get out of it what you put into it. As John puts it, 'All you can do is work like hell, since this might be your only chance'. I felt it was like holding a tiger by the tail—if we let go, our life savings would be swallowed up.

By the end of those first two years, we had a reasonable dealership going, but I was close to snapping under the strain of spending all my free time down at the laboratory after work had finished in the City. I decided to pull out of accountancy altogether. But the question remained: could we get our back-street company onto a really viable basis?

We began to find the answer by moving into colour processing. Before 1967 we had sub-contracted all our colour work to Cooper & Pearson. That year we decided that Grunwick should do the work itself. The catch was that the equipment we needed cost about £20,000 and we had no cash. I persuaded Johnsons of Hendon, who were keen to sell colour processing equipment, to sell us the machines we needed without any personal guarantees. I also sent John Hickey off for one afternoon a week to Harrow Technical College to learn about colour processing.

We needed more than one garage to house our miniature technological revolution. I managed to lease the garage across the road from us, which we turned into an office, and a third a few doors away, which gave us additional space for processing. In the years that followed we moved up and down the mews as other tenants moved out. We went upstairs, downstairs and all over the place. The properties in the street were owned by the Council, which proved to be a tolerant landlord. We would knock down the walls of adjacent houses to give ourselves bigger rooms to work in. Our only real problem was the neighbours, some of whom would complain when the machines were whirring away in the dead of night, especially since we could not afford air conditioning and would keep the doors open in summer to make the workrooms a bit cooler.

We began to make some real money, charging about two shillings for a colour print. But we were reaching the point where a bigger decision had to be taken: whether we would base our further expansion on dealing only with chemists and shops, or also offer processing services through the mail order business. I had heard of a firm in Glasgow which gave away free films and dealt directly with the public. This sounded like a good idea, as it would enable us to receive films from all over the country and therefore offered us the advantages of economies of size not hitherto possible.

Bonuspool was launched in 1968, with advertisements placed in the *Daily Express* and the *Daily Mirror*. We anticipated that these advertisements would bring in a considerable number of films. Precisely two black and white films were received in response. It looked as if the new company was a disaster.

We then tried advertising in a specialist magazine, *Amateur Photographer*. This did not work particularly well either.

I went over to the United States in the autumn of 1969 to find out more about mail order techniques. I learnt that the key lay in direct mailing: the mass distribution of evelopes throughout the country. A printer was persuaded to produce,

on credit, a lot of American-style envelopes, with red, white
and blue stripes; the text on the red band showed what was
saved compared with shop prices, and the text on the blue
band showed prices charged. A distributor was then found,
again on credit, to do a test mailing of two million envelopes
in London and the Home Counties distributing pre-paid
envelopes for return. It was a gamble that paid off: the orders
came flooding in.

The economics of the exercise were very simple. Instead of
giving a trade discount to retail photographic outlets, we
could give a direct benefit to the customer by supplying him
with a free replacement film. We were basically no worse off
in doing this than if we were dealing with the shops, while the
customer stood to gain. People would put their money and
film in the pre-paid envelope and send it back for processing.
Their developed prints would be returned to them plus the
free film. If they continued sending their films for processing
by mail order, they would never have to buy another film
again. As the retail trading side had become highly
competitive, with even larger discounts being offered to
outlets to secure their business, the free film mail order
business was more secure in that price cutting was not
possible without mounting a similar big marketing operation.

After this, Grunwick went from strength to strength. The
format of the envelopes was improved by stressing feminine
colours—pastels like pink and lavender—to appeal to the
housewife. We learned a lot about presentation from a female
marketing director in America. Another lesson learnt in
America is that money can be made by giving credits. If a
customer was supposed to be charged £2 for having twenty
prints developed, but only eighteen were worth developing, a
credit would be given for two extra prints—another way of
ensuring that the next film came back to us.

Malcolm Alden had, by now, joined the Company in the
capacity of a Computer Manager as we had decided to
computerise our accountancy records from simple ledger
posting machines. At this stage the main problem was to find
a place to house the computer, as we had again run out of

space in Loudoun Road Mews. By a bizarre coincidence, the elderly man living in the flat above us fell asleep and set his flat on fire. A director and one of our staff broke down the door and managed to get him out. The Council rehoused him, but his flat was partly gutted. We were able to rent it to house our new computer, which had to be swung in through the first floor window.

As Bonuspool's turnover expanded, an even riskier mail order venture named Trucolor was launched in 1974. This was based on the 'pay later' principle, under which the customer received an invoice with his completed order. It had to be possible to check on who were paying their bills, and this involved us in changing our small computer for a more powerful one with disc packs and magnetic tape peripherals to cope with the increased workload. Enormous problems with this new more sophisticated computer lay ahead.

At the end of 1973 we merged with the old-established family firm of Cooper & Pearson. Both of us needed to expand and to invest in new technology, and we had been working together well in the past; we decided to pool our resources and form a holding company. The mail order side of the business was growing from day to day, and although we had moved into a new factory in Cobbold Road, Willesden, we still did not have enough space. So we rented the thirteenth floor of Station House in Wembley on a short lease and put our Mail Order Department and the new computer up there.

The trouble was that the systems for the new computer did not work. Theoretically, it was a beautiful set-up, rather like the system used by many airlines to check reservations, in which a girl can type the details of an invoice and they show up on a kind of television screen. We found out too late that the software that we would need to make the necessary modifications to our computer system would take another seven man years to produce. It was supposed to be operational by April 1974, when it was planned to send out another mass distribution of envelopes. It was not.

Urgent instructions were sent to the distributor not to go

ahead with the mailing, but it was too late. The envelopes went out, and the work came flooding in. Before we knew it, we had 200,000 orders stacked to the ceiling in Station House which we could not dispatch, since we could not produce invoices for them. This was one of those times when your stomach really gets knotted up.

I called everyone together to discover a solution, and some of the managers seemed to be on the verge of a nervous breakdown. We finally got round the problem by short-circuiting the whole system and reverting to a simple batch system of invoicing which had been used successfully in the past. But we still ran into enormous difficulties. Just when we had almost got things sorted out our printers managed to duplicate our order books, so that we had two lots of identical order numbers. This completely baffled our computer.

These shortcomings with the new computer were eventually overcome, but they lost the Company an awful lot of money. Fortunately, the year 1975/76 was one of the best ever. In retrospect, our crisis in 1974 was a good educational experience. Once again, we had to work extremely long hours, and I remember seeing the dawn come up on several mornings. The managers and workforce had learnt to work together through this crisis, which left us a very hardened team, able to compete effectively in the photo-finishing industry, and to make Grunwick one of the most successful companies in its field. The crisis left us with the feeling that we need fear no one in the industry and could compete with anyone. In this sense, it was very good training for the political storms that were to break later on.

The company's success had already been recognised in a survey of colour processing that was published in the consumer magazine, *Which* in June 1972. The *Which* report concluded that Bonuspool was the best buy for film processing in the country. In a later survey, published in June 1977, *Which* concluded that we had maintained our standards. This later *Which* report also noted that the Bonuspool service was much faster than any competing mail order scheme.

As Grunwick had expanded, so had the staff. Interestingly, we had no labour troubles in either the Loudoun Road Mews premises or in Station House, Wembley—despite the fact that conditions were often very trying in both locations. For example, the Loudoun Road Mews premises were in a cobbled street, and very unhygienic. The buildings were rickety, and I had to have three buckets in my own office to catch the constant drip of water from the leaking roof. There were rats around. We only had old fashioned gas heaters for warmth in winter, and because the laboratories were scattered through several houses and garages, the staff had to carry the film back and forth through rain and sleet.

But we had no problems with unions or political activists in those days. Our only significant labour problem was with drug addicts, in an area that was noted for hippies at the time. Our workforce in St John's Wood was mainly white, with one or two Asians.

Conditions at Station House were also far from perfect. The building had no air conditioning apart from the computer suite itself, and since it was almost completely sheathed in plate glass the heat in the summer was almost intolerable. We did not even have our own lavatories; our employees had to go outside our part of the building to use communal facilities. We soon found that some of them were using this for various extra-curricular activities. Complaints were made to us about certain members of our staff (who, incidentally, no longer work for us) who were going into unoccupied floors to make love. When this came to light we insisted for a few days that employees should seek permission to leave the company premises. This was the origin of the myth that workers had to put their hands up to go to the lavatory.

Conditions were very much better at the Cobbold Road works and also at Chapter Road where we came to occupy two premises, the Cooper & Pearson works which the combined company continued to occupy after our merger with them, and another factory which we leased from the Brent Council and on which we had to spend £70,000 to modernise it and make it comfortable. Ironically, when conditions improved for the staff, the labour troubles began.

I was not conscious of the reputation of the Brent area for left-wing activism when we decided to move into the Cobbold Road plant from Loudoun Road Mews at the beginning of 1972. It is no mystery to me now that (according to surveys prepared by the Brent Trades Council and Union of Post Office Workers) there had been a notable exodus of small businesses from this corner of north-west London in recent years. Still one of London's major industrial areas, the Brent district has become a stamping-ground for left-wing militants. Still, there was no indication that Grunwick would be singled out as a target until early in 1973.

On my return from a holiday that January, I was met at the airport by my sister Jean. Before we had even got into her car, she had broken the news that a letter had been sent to the company by a Mr Cosgrove, the district organiser of the Transport and General Workers' Union. He had demanded to meet the Grunwick management to discuss union recognition, claiming that the TGWU had already recruited 'a considerable number' of our employees. It later transpired that five of our employees had been recruited by the TGWU in the winter of 1972; several others were said to be interested. There was no evidence that the TGWU had any appreciable support at the time, and we decided to pay little attention to Mr Cosgrove's letter.

Not long afterwards, we were obliged to make three of our employees redundant. This provided the pretext for a walk-out. Contrary to later propaganda, no one was sacked for joining, or trying to join, a union. The simple fact was that work was short, to the point when some of the workers in the black-and-white department were taking two hour lunch breaks on the grounds that they did not have enough work to do. It was revealing that the two workers who were left managed to cope with the entire workload that had been handled by eight people before. When we announced the redundancies, four other employees in this department decided to walk out. In all, fifteen of our workers walked out on 15 January.

The TGWU appeared on the scene, and we found ourselves involved in a union dispute. The workers who had been made redundant turned out to be union members, as were the people who walked out in sympathy with them, but this was most certainly not the reason they were made redundant. Indeed at the time we had no means of knowing who was or was not a union member. This was the basis for the later propaganda claim that was finally scotched in the evidence presented during the Scarman hearings—that Grunwick had sacked people in 1973 for joining a union.

Many of the characters who became familiar in the course of the later picketing turned up during this earlier dispute. Notable among them was Tom Durkin, the chairman of Brent Trades Council, a veteran left-winger. He played a key role in organising picketing outside the gates at Cobbold Road. We were warned that we were opposing Britain's strongest trade union and could not possibly hold out against it.

The strike organisers in 1973 introduced some of the themes that were developed in 1976 and 1977. Roneoed leaflets were put out by a body that called itself the 'Grunwick Laboratories' Workers' Action Committee', claiming that the dispute revolved around 'the right to join a trade union of one's choice'. I was described as a reactionary employer who treated his employees as 'sub-humans'. Workers were mobilised from nearby factories like Mulliner Park Ward, a subsidiary of Rolls Royce which produces the Camargue and Corniche models, to join the picket line. But the picketing ended with a whimper.

Less than two weeks after one of the picket leaders had claimed that the men outside Cobbold Road were ready to continue the struggle 'indefinitely', the strikers threw in the sponge. Apart from the fact that we were not willing to give way, the pickets were demoralised by the fact that the union did not make the strike official—perhaps because it was unsure of its own case. This also explains why strike pay was not paid on the lavish scale that became familiar later on. Finally, the strike took place in winter, which meant not only that the picket lines were an unpleasant place to be, but that the company was coasting through the slack season. Significantly, later industrial disruption was initiated at the height of our busiest season, around the time of the August bank holiday.

The rights and wrongs of the 1973 dispute can be gauged from the findings of the industrial tribunal which heard the appeals of five of the workers who had been dismissed. The Tribunal (which included a union representative) ruled unanimously that Grunwick's action had been entirely justified. Four of the workers who appealed had been in employment for an insufficient length of time to be qualified to claim unfair dismissal, so that the question of whether we had got rid of employees for being union members had to be settled on the basis of the fifth case, that of an Irishwoman called Breda Mulvey. The tribunal found that she had been fairly dismissed and that there was no evidence that the management had ever been aware that she had joined the TGWU. 'We feel bound to come to the conclusion,' the tribunal noted, 'that the principle reason for her dismissal was not the fact that she was a union member or was exercising rights in relation thereto.'

So much for the myth that I have always been an employer who sacks workers simply because they wish to join a union. In 1973, as in 1976, I acted as any responsible employer would have felt obliged to do in dismissing workers who joined in a strike in breach of their contracts, and some of whom took part in disorderly picketing and in circulating unsubstantiated and inflammatory reports about my company.

I am convinced that Grunwick's success in withstanding the strike of 1973 made us a major target for the left-wing union organisers in the Brent area. Tom Durkin insisted in his testimony at the Scarman hearings that this episode had inspired a 'very bitter' reaction throughout the trade union movement in north-west London. I believe that Durkin and his friends were determined to have their revenge. But it took another three years before they were organised to make a major onslaught on Grunwick.

4

The air-conditioned sweatshop

If you go by the union propaganda, you would imagine that
Grunwick exists to exploit immigrant workers as slave labour.
No one who has ever been inside the company could honestly
defend this picture of it. For a start, the immigrant question
has been grossly exaggerated. After we moved to Willesden,
it is true that we took on a high proportion of coloured
immigrant workers. This was not the result of a deliberate
policy of picking cheap labour; it was a result of the different
social composition of Willesden and the St John's Wood area
where we had previously worked. I have always tried to
ensure that no one would be refused a job because of his race,
colour or origin. The recruiting policy of Grunwick and the
associate companies has been open; we do not discriminate
against or in favour of any group.

I have also always tried to ensure that no one's oppor-
tunities were limited because of his race or background.
There were, and are, a number of coloured managers at the
company, and the first manager we ever appointed was a
Ugandan Asian, who still works for us, Johnny Kassam.
Grunwick's workforce is truly multiracial, and includes West
Indians, Africans, Indians, Irish, English, Scots, Poles,
Fijians, East Germans, Mauritian Chinese, Ugandan Asians
and Kenyan Asians, amongst others. Our philosophy has
always been to encourage our employees to give the company
the best they can, and in return to give them the rewards that
they earn. By the same token, we expect of ourselves to give
eveything we can to our work, and by so doing we hope to set
a good example to those who work for us.

I have always liked to run my business from 'up front'. I
like to deal with staff individually and to make myself
available to them whenever they want to see me. I always

make a point of being personally involved in arranging the traditional Christmas bonuses. I feel strongly that, in a small business, industrial relations are best conducted directly between the workforce and their management, rather than by the introduction of outside forces. At Grunwick the management consults with the workforce through an elected Works Committee. The Works Committee, first established in 1973, was not designed as an alternative to direct contact between workers and management, but as a supplement to it. Again, anyone who has visited Chapter Road and Cobbold Road knows that managers (and directors) are not loftily removed from the workforce, but sit in glassed-in offices in full view of them. There is nothing remote about management at Grunwick: could the same be said of most bigger firms?

Despite what has been said about me, I have never been anti-union in the sense that I would have any objection to any of our workers joining a union if they chose to do so. I would say frankly that, even prior to the Grunwick dispute, I had seen plenty of evidence that unions càn cause unnecessary problems. It had seemed to me for years that the modern trend in trade unionism has been to move further and further away from the original justification for the organisation of labour. At the outset, trade unions played an indispensable role in helping individual workers to improve their pay and conditions. But in Britain in recent times, it has become clear that the major unions are politically motivated and have little concern for the lot of the individual worker, still less for that of the community as a whole.

In some industries, the power of big unions is so great that workers are required to owe their primary allegiance to the union rather than to the company. I cannot believe that this is good for business, for the country, or for the long-term prosperity of the workers themselves. It is clear that the majority of rank and file union members do not support militant leadership; but, regrettably, in any organised movement it is a few people who rule the roost.

Apart from the clash with the TGWU in 1973, we had no

trouble with the unions until we moved to Chapter Road. Ironically, we were inclined at first to think that this move would be an answer to all our problems. Conditions at Station House were fairly rough; as I mentioned earlier, it was the fact that we did not even have our own toilet facilities that led to the widely-circulated myth about employees having to put up their hands to go to the lavatories. At Chapter Road we had our own canteen, and toilet facilities, and no problem about getting up to the thirteenth floor—everything was on the ground floor. We spent a lot of money doing up the Chapter Road works. The only thing that was not working properly at the beginning of that long hot summer of 1976 was the refrigeration part of the air-conditioning. The ventilation part was working, but the air cooling system had not been deliverd by the manufacturers when we moved in.

That summer started out no different from any other summer. Perhaps the only notable change was that there was not so much overtime for our part-time students to do, which made them rather unhappy, since they could earn more money by working longer hours. In contrast to the fairy stories about Grunwick, it was the relative lack of over-time—rather than an excess of 'compulsory' overtime—that may have contributed to bad feelings that summer.

There may have been one other source of grievance, which was the fact that some of the people who had worked for us at Station House resented having to travel further to get to Dollis Hill; our nearest tube station. This applied, for example, to Mrs Desai, who became a figurehead for the pickets, who told us that she wanted a special bus laid on to bring her over from Wembley.

It is true that everyone was expected to work hard during the three or four summer months, late June to early October. Photo-finishing, in relation to the annual cycle, is like harvesting. It is a seasonal thing, and more than half of our turnover depends on what we do in one third of the year. Our policy was to keep a fairly large permanent staff throughout the year, rather than providing fewer full-time jobs and taking on more part-time workers when the pressure was on.

This meant that our workers had a pretty easy ride through the autumn and winter months. The pickets who later made a song and dance about compulsory overtime in summer did not tell the public the important thing—that everyone understood that the company's success depended on extra work through the summer, that the need to work overtime was fully explained to them in advance and was indeed written into their contracts of employment. Life was very much more casual through the rest of the year, and no one who wanted a straightforward nine to five job should go to work for Grunwick.

A lot of nonsense was also talked about wage levels at Grunwick. The unions were always trying to make out that we paid our staff at starvation rates. According to the strike bulletins and the APEX propaganda, we were paying our permanent staff £28 for a forty-hour week and £25 for a thirty-five-hour week at the time the strike began in August 1976. In fact, these were merely the basic rates for trainees. Out of 239 permanent staff working a basic forty-hour week at the beginning of August, only 22 were on the minimum rate of £28 (which of course does not include overtime). Out of 103 permanent staff working a basic thirty-five-hour week only 21 were paid the minimum rate of £25. I do not dispute that these starting rates are not high, but they must be considered in relation to what is paid by comparable companies in a highly competitive industry. For experienced process workers, our rates of pay varied between £35 and £60 for a forty-hour week at the time the dispute started.

If anyone objects that *all* workers in photo-finishing should be paid more, I would say: I agree completely. But if you depend on the market, you can only pay what the market allows. If our customers are willing to pay more for their processed film, we can pay higher wages. If they are not, our choice is either to keep wages at an economic level or to try to reduce the size of our workforce by increased productivity. The only alternative to this is to make a loss, which would force the company to close. This is primary school economics. But it seems that there are many people on the left who think they can suspend the laws of supply and demand—perhaps because the Labour Government has done this so frequently in the case of nationalised industries and other Bennite hobby-horses.

Grunwick wage rates in August 1976 were comparable to or better than rates paid by similar laboratories in London, and significantly higher than those in a comparable photo-finishing laboratory in Leicester where APEX is recognised—even when allowance was made for the difference in wage rates between London and the provinces. We presented evidence to this effect at the Scarman inquiry (of which more anon). Unfortunately, that inquiry declined to take evidence from a neutral expert, Mr Edward Southey of the Photographic Careers Centre, which provides staff for the whole of the photographic industry (and has never done work for Grunwick). But in his prepared statement, Mr Southey said that the average pay for a trainee in the photographic industry as a whole was only £22 for a 37½ hour week. He rejected comparisons between Grunwick and big companies like Kodak, Ilford and Technicolor. He pointed out that a company like Kodak, as a manufacturer operating in a monopoly market, can easily pass on the cost of high wages to the consumer. In any case, Kodak's income mostly stems from producing materials and equipment, and photo-finishing is a relatively minor aspect of its overall operations, while Ilford does not have a photo-finishing operation at all. Technicolor specialises in processing movie film.

Mr Southey also found that working conditions at Grunwick's premises at both Chapter Road and Cobbold Road were 'well above average', as were its canteen and ventilation facilities. You could get a cup of tea for 2p, a pie for 10p and a complete lunch for about 20p in our canteen.

No company offers ideal conditions. But Grunwick was a dynamic firm with spotless modern premises, complete with piped music, its own canteen, and air-conditioning. A worker who disliked the pay or conditions was under no compulsion to stay there. Far from being a wicked exploiter, Grunwick was serving the country well by offering jobs in a depressed area with high unemployment, and by bringing in export income. No doubt there are always grievances; but it seems to me that the industrial conflict that has raged around Grunwick has its roots, not in the pay and conditions at our firm, but in efforts to exploit minor personal problems for political ends.

5

The walk-out

The storm broke in the summer of 1976, in the middle of our peak season when holiday films are pouring in from all over the country. It began on the day I went off on holiday to Ireland: Friday, 20 August. I knew nothing about the dispute until the following Tuesday, when my younger son rushed into the bedroom first thing in the morning and told me 'Dad, did you know you had got a strike on at your company?' It seemed that John Hickey had phoned the previous evening and that my sister Jean had taken the call; she had been told there had been a mass walk-out, and that some of the staff had rioted and smashed windows. I telephoned John at once; he told me that things were looking ugly.

But I decided to let my family (including my invalid mother) enjoy their full fortnight's holiday, and did not return to London until 5 September. Some people seem to have found this surprising. My reason for staying away was not that I underestimated the scale of the dispute—although no one could have foretold that it was to grow to the proportions it later assumed—but that I had full confidence in my fellow directors and the young executives to whom I had been delegating more and more of the workload over the previous year. My account of what happened in those first two weeks is based on what I have learned from the workers, managers and directors who were there at the time.

There were two separate incidents in the mail order department at Chapter Road on 20 August. The first involved a nineteen-year-old boy called Devshi Bhudia, who came to England in 1974. As he was leaving his office for lunch at about 1 p.m. that Friday, Malcolm Alden noticed that there were about thirteen crates of completed work that remained to be dealt with in the sorting area of his department. He asked Devshi Bhudia, whose job was to sort the packets of work before they were invoiced and prepared for mailing, how long he thought it would take him to sort out a single crate. He said that he could sort a crate in five minutes. Malcolm Alden told him that he would need the thirteen crates to be processed by 2 p.m. by the five people who were working with Bhudia. This was hardly a tall order. The reason for setting a deadline was that at this stage of our peak season huge backlogs of work can build up fast unless we keep to a tight schedule.

Later that afternoon, at about 3.30 p.m., Malcolm was talking to Ken Pearson when he noticed that the thirteen crates had not been touched. Bhudia was working in slow motion. Malcolm considered that the manner in which he was carrying out—or rather not carrying out—his work was insolent and provocative, since both Ken and Malcolm were standing only a few feet away from him and could obviously see what was going on.

Ken felt, like Malcolm, that Bhudia was trying to make some kind of point. After Ken left the Chapter Road premises, Malcolm asked Bhudia to go into his office and asked him why he was not working properly. Bhudia said that he would work faster if he was paid more. At this time, Bhudia was earning a basic £29 for a thirty-five-hour week, not counting the overtime that he was paid on top of that. In the course of their conversation, Bhudia repeatedly said to Malcolm 'I know you want to sack me.' He then challenged Malcolm to sack him. Malcolm responded by suggesting that Bhudia should leave the premises at once and accept one week's wages in lieu of notice.

Malcolm says that after Bhudia left his office, he heard him say 'OK boys, this is it.' Bhudia left the premises on his own, but a few minutes later three of his colleagues, two of them students working during the summer vacation, told Malcolm that they wanted to leave too. They then walked out and stayed outside the main gates at Chapter Road.

Significantly, in his testimony to the Scarman Court of Inquiry, Bhudia admitted that he had already secured

another job at Smiths Industries, and that they were going to
pay him £41 for a thirty-seven-hour week. He also admitted
that he had arranged with his colleagues in the sorting section
that if he were dismissed they would walk out too. He denied
that he said anything to them, but did concede that he picked
up his newspaper, which might be construed as a signal.

It was already clear that there was an element of
premeditation in what was happening on that Friday. This
became clearer from the second incident, involving Mrs
Jayaben Desai. Just before 6 p.m. Peter Diffey noticed that
Mrs Desai was preparing to go home. He asked her what she
was doing. She said that the staff were all getting ready to go
home, and that was what she intended to do. Peter pointed
out that nobody was about to leave, and that there was a good
half hour's work to do before anyone would be going home.
Since she had worked in the mail order department for two
years, Mrs Desai must have been fully aware that it was
always the company's policy to despatch all outstanding
processed work on a Friday evening during the summer
months before any of the staff left the premises. Peter asked
Mrs Desai to spend the remaining time checking lists of
payments received from customers. This was not an unusual
request, since Mrs Desai often did this kind of work.

But Mrs Desai gave vent to a torrent of abuse, shouting in
Gujerati about the management. Several of our workers in
the mail order department later said that they thought that
Mrs Desai had exploded in this way because Malcolm Alden
had rebuked her son early that afternoon, when he was
fooling around noisily with a friend of his. Bipin Patel, a
student employed in the department, says that after Malcolm
told off Sunil Desai, Sunil was extremely angry, and told
Bipin that when he left the company in 'about a week's time',
he was definitely going 'to create a scene'.

Malcolm Alden came out of his office when the shouting
began. He was surprised by what was happening, since Mrs
Desai had worked at the company for about two years and
had been a reasonable if limited worker. Becuse of the noise,
Malcolm asked both Peter and Mrs Desai to go into his office

so they could talk things over. Mrs Desai at first refused, and only finally agreed to go after yelling at Malcolm as well. She became increasingly hysterical, shouting in both English and Gujerati. She yelled in English that she wanted her 'freedom' and asked for her cards. Malcolm said that, in view of her behaviour, we would not try to persuade her to stay. She stormed out of Peter's office and started yelling at the staff in the open plan office immediately outside.

Her son, Sunil, a student who was working with the temporary staff in the mail order department, then leapt up from his desk and shouted that he was also going to leave the company. The two of them stood in the middle of the floor like soap box orators. 'Can't you understand what these managers are doing to us?' Mrs Desai demanded. Malcolm requested them to leave the premises, and eventually he and Peter escorted them to the main gates. They joined Devshi Bhudia and the sorters who had walked out earlier and remained outside.

This was the prelude to the battle of Grunwick. The Scarman report concluded that there was an element of 'premeditation' in Devshi Bhudia's departure, but that Mrs Desai's departure was spontaneous. However, Bhudia's group were waiting outside when Mrs Desai and her son Sunil walked out. But the most striking thing is that there had been no mention of a trade union up to this point.

On Friday night, and over the weekend, the people who had walked out met with their friends and prepared for the mass walk-out that took place on Monday 23 August. As the staff arrived at the main gates of Chapter Road that morning, they were met by Mrs Desai and her friends. Mrs Desai urged the staff to come out on strike, and asked them to put their names and addresses on a piece of paper, which many of them did. The paper was blank, and when Azadi Patel asked what it was all about, she was simply told that it was 'about the union'.

Jessie Patel, one of our supervisors, said to Mrs Desai that she would not put her signature on plain paper—she must have some writing on it. Mrs Desai told her that she would 'write on it later' but Jessie refused to sign. Most of those who did sign had no idea what they were putting their names to. Perhaps Mrs Desai herself did not know either, since APEX had not yet appeared on the scene. It was this blank piece of paper, by the way, that was described in the Scarman report as 'a document in support of a union'. It was never produced to the enquiry for inspection.

During the teabreak and lunchbreak, the pickets lobbied the Chapter Road staff to join in a mass walk-out at 3 p.m. The presence of press photographers when it took place suggests a certain degree of organisation. At 3 p.m. Malcolm Alden noticed that many of the staff in the mail order department were leaving their places of work and going outside. He asked several of them if they knew what they were doing, but received no coherent reply. Sunil Desai was outside in the yard, calling on our employees to walk out and shouting 'Remember your Marxism.' About fifty-two people joined the walk-out from Chapter Road, and began to march down to the other plant in Cobbold Road, about half a mile away.

John Hickey jumped into his car and drove round to Cobbold Road to warn the managers of what was happening. Trevor Salmon, one of the managers at Cobbold Road who is nicknamed 'Kojak' by the staff, dashed round to the entrance of the estate to see what was happening. As soon as the crowd from Chapter Road saw him, there was no chance of discussion. They began to shout, scream, swear and spit, and he had to run back down the road to reach the building before they did. There was no time to lock the main doors and about twenty people from Chapter Road milled around the staff and reception entrances. A number of them managed to get through into the clocking-in area, where Ken Pearson and several managers were standing. It took some time before they could be made to leave and the doors could be locked.

A riot quickly developed. One woman tried to climb through a window into one of the offices and had to be shoved back. People ran back and forth along the side of the building, smashing reinforced windows and hacking at doors with sticks, iron bars and heavy plastic tubing.

Inside the Cobbold Road plant, the strikers had sympathisers. The most aggressive was Kantilal Patel, the senior continuous-film processor, who subsequently threatened me with a brick on the picket lines. We had been having problems with Kantilal, who sometimes came back from lunch visibly the worse for drink, although he was basically a competent worker. I don't know whether he also suffered from some illness but he fainted twice in the darkroom for no apparent reason during the time that he was employed by us and had to be sent to hospital for examination. He also complained, on occasions, of severe headaches. He was a bit of a bully boy inside the works, and he showed his mettle that Monday. Ken Pearson saw him pushing people physically out of the door, including two film processors, Nilesh Ruperalia and Rajandra Pandya, who were clearly unwilling to leave. He tried, but failed, to push Arvind Patel, one of our most loyal employees, out the door.

I had another brush with Kantilal Patel later on, which gave rise to the famous story of how the management had tried to beat up one of the pickets. This occurred when I had driven into the Chapter Road plant at lunchtime one day in March to prepare for some visitors we were expecting from Holland. As I parked my car, I noticed that Kantilal was on company property. I told him to get off, quite politely, then turned my back on him and walked towards the office door.

He followed me into the front office where I was hit by him at the side of my head which left me streaming with blood, since he wears a heavy signet ring. I defended myself, while calling for assistance. he staggered back against a water fountain, which he seized upon with the obvious intent of trying to throw it at me. I managed to pin him down, although he was struggling like a wild animal; alternately still and violent. Finally our personnel manager, Norman Woollett, came to my help and shunted Kantilal towards the gates.

Jack Dromey managed to drag him off eventually but not before Kantilal had succeeded in delivering two smart kicks to my groin when he rushed onto the property on seeing me cross the company yard. This episode confirmed my original impression that, with Kantilal, we were not dealing with someone who believed entirely in peaceful and rational persuasion.

A total of 137 people joined the walk-out in that last week in August—91 of them permanent staff, and 46 student workers who were due to go back to their studies within a week or so in any case. Many people appear to find it hard to believe that so many of our workers could have joined the strike if there had not been deep-seated grievances. Yet, despite repeated enquiries, no real grievances have ever been put forward: those that have been raised by the pickets and their supporters have in every single instance turned out to be unfounded.

One important factor which most people tend to underrate is the extraordinary importance of family and personal ties among the Asian community. There is no doubt in my mind, or in the minds of most of the workers that I have talked to, that sympathy for Jayaben Desai and Devshi Bhudia was the key element in the walk-out. In the Ugandan Asian community, age brings respect. Mrs Desai was one of the older people employed by Grunwick and was therefore accepted as a natural leader. She had a number of friends from the same area who were all loyal to her, and it was these friends and associates who led the walk-out. Similarly, the personal link between Devshi Bhudia and Kantilal Patel helps to explain why workers from Cobbold Road joined a strike that began in the mail department in Chapter Road. Kantilal Patel was an orphan who had close connections with Bhudia's family. When Bhudia walked out, he automatically felt personally involved.

I do not believe that even half the people who walked out of Grunwick knew at the outset what they were doing. The line that was being put across to them was 'We'll tell you what it's all about when you get outside'. Once outside, they tended to stay outside. Of course, I was not present at the time, but the accounts of those who were present tend to bear this out.

Bipin Patel, for example, testified to the Scarman court that the organisers of the walk-out on Monday were going round asking people to join the strike without giving any reason whatsoever for it. All that one of them, Miss Rajeshwari Patel, could say by way of explanation was that 'Someone has asked me to spread it around.' Even the ringleaders seem to have had a less than clear idea about what they were doing.

Kantilal Patel later phoned Ken Pearson and told him that he felt that Devshi Bhudia had been treated badly. Ken replied that he did not think that Kantilal understood the full facts of the dismissal, and suggested that he checked his information with Bhudia. A week or so later, Kantilal phoned Ken again and told him that he had talked with Bhudia and established that what Ken had told him about the dismissal was true. He said that because of his personal circumstances, he had thought that he had to support Bhudia on the Monday of the walk-out and that, despite the fact that Bhudia had misled him, he would have to go on supporting the strike.

The supposed 'slave labour' conditions at Grunwick, as shown in the last chapter (and as conceded by the Scarman report) were a figment of the imagination of people who subsequently sought to exploit the dispute for their own political aims. Once they became directly involved, the shapeless riot of Monday 23 August assumed a new and ominous character.

6

Enter the union

The union that latched on to the Grunwick dispute is one that has claimed credit in the past for its supposed moderation and might seem to have little in common with the unskilled and semi-skilled process workers it is trying to recruit, since the bulk of its members are engineers. Its involvement was almost accidental. It had little in common with the hard left-wingers on the Brent Trades Council to whom it lent its name and relative respectability. It appeared to have nothing at all in common with the Grunwick strikers.

APEX is a white-collar union with some 143,000 members, 90,000 of whom are in the engineering industry. APEX has frequently argued that it is a 'moderate' union with no interest, for example, in imposing the closed shop if it won recognition at Grunwick. Such assurances have to be measured against the record of how APEX has insisted on compulsory unionisation in the past.

A case in point is that of Mr Peter Thickpenny, a clerical assistant at Perkins Diesel Engine Company in Peterborough, who was sacked in May 1976 for refusing to join APEX, which had established a closed shop at the company. He had two small children and had just come out of hospital after several days of tests for a severe heart condition. Mr Thickpenny was quoted in *The Times* after his dismissal as saying 'I am sticking to my principles that it is every man's right to join a union or not. I have made my decision although I have a mortgage to pay and a family to support.' I would not wish anyone who worked for us ever to find himself in a similar position. It is a curious kind of 'moderation' on the part of a union that makes it possible.

There are other examples of how APEX has pushed for the closed shop. After twenty-eight years of loyal service with

Lawrence Scott Electronics in Bredbury, Cheshire, Mr John Jeffrey was sacked after APEX managed to obtain a closed shop there. Mr Jeffrey did not wish to join APEX and was sacked after APEX members refused to work with him. Management at the factory had been willing to discuss a hundred per cent union membership agreement, so long as it included safeguards for long-serving employees who might not wish to join. APEX, however, as works manager Douglas Astbury stated, tried 'to force it upon us'. Consequently, another worker who dared to exercise his right not to be press-ganged into the union ranks was thrown out of work.

At the time that APEX intervened at Grunwick, it had no members in the film processing industry. At the time that it declared the strike official its general secretary, Roy Grantham, seems to have had only a flimsy command of the facts. For example, he had received an internal memo from his regional organiser, Len Gristey on 31 August that claimed that there had been a walk-out of 200 workers from Grunwick. The real figure was 137. But it is important to note that when APEX became involved, so did the Labour government. Denis Howell, a government minister, is also the president of APEX.

Was it an accident or a bureaucratic oversight that directed the strike leaders to APEX rather than some other union? Was it felt by those who advised them that, after the failure of the TGWU in the 1973 dispute, they should go to some other union? I cannot answer these questions. But the role of APEX was to show that, when the status of a union is at stake, 'moderates' can be as militant as anyone.

Sunil Desai told the Grunwick workers whom he met in the park during the lunch hour on Monday 23 August that he had set up a meeting with a union official for the following day. He had gone along to the Citizens' Advice Bureau in Brent, which suggested that the strikers should contact 'the TUC', and gave them a telephone number. They made the call, and were advised that a suitable union for them to approach was APEX. They also got in touch with the Brent Community Law Centre, where Jack Dromey is employed.

They were passed on to the Brent Trades Council, where he wears his other hat as Secretary to this Trade Council. Dromey became the key adviser to the strikers.

On Tuesday night, Len Gristey, the senior London organiser of APEX, Jack Dromey and sixty or seventy strikers turned up for a meeting at the Brent Trades and Labour Hall. Many of them applied that night to become members of APEX, and the union executive council decided to give them retrospective membership. By the end of the first week, the 91 permanent staff who had joined the strike had been made members of APEX.

Union recognition, which was totally unrelated to the original dispute, now became its focus. Len Gristey met Ken Pearson and John Stacey our personnel manager in the road outside the Cobbold Road factory that Friday, and Gristey told them that he was having great trouble controlling the religious leaders of the Asian community at Southall, and that they were planning to march on the factory during the bank holiday weekend. Gristey said that he did not think he could stop them doing this. Ken interpreted this as a threat. The same day, Gristey wrote to the company, formally requesting that we should recognise Apex as the appropriate union to deal with the affairs of the staff. He suggested a meeting 'to discuss a detailed recognition and procedure agreement'.

Before they had received a written response from us (their letter only reached us on 31 August, because of the bank holiday delay in the post) Mr Gristey and his chief, Roy Grantham, had, in their own words, come to the conclusion that they were dealing with an 'obdurate' employer. They declared the strike official, and started paying the pickets strike pay.

We were not overly impressed by APEX's claim to have a legitimate interest in our affairs. APEX had only appeared on the scene after the dispute began. No Grunwick worker was a member of APEX at the time of the walk-out. I regarded APEX as entirely irrelevant to the problem.

While I was away, John Hickey consulted our solicitors

about where we stood in relation to the people who had walked out and taken part in the riot. The legal position was absolutely clear, although it may seem surrealistic to those who do not understand the convoluted prose of the Employment Protection Act. The company was advised on 1 September that under the curious provisions of this act we had only two real options. We must either take all the pickets back, or sack them all. If we took even one of them back, we would be liable for a whole series of actions against us for unfair dismissal, on the grounds that we had discriminated in favour of some strikers against others. Even if we were able to win each legal action that might be brought against us, the cost of the court cases could be stupendous.

The decision that had to be taken, on the basis of this advice, was a very painful one. It was clear to our board that many of the Grunwick workers who joined the picket lines had done so under pressure, or because they were totally ignorant of what was actually happening. It was sad for us to have to conclude that we had no option but to dismiss all the pickets for industrial misconduct.

APEX claimed that we sacked people for joining a trade union. They could have put this claim to a legal test by summoning the Company, under Section 78 of the Employment Protection Act 1975, to a Special Tribunal hearing to defend itself against this charge, which would have amounted to unfair dismissals should the case have been proved. They never took this action. Obviously they did not believe their own propaganda.

At the subsequent Industrial Tribunal hearings held in connection with these dismissals it was unanimously held by the members of the Tribunal, one of whom was a Trade Union member, that the Company had acted completely within the law in dismissing those people who had walked out.

I returned to the company on 7 September. I had remained closely in touch with the situation by telephone, and was glad, on balance, that I had stuck to my original decision not to return early from holiday. This might have suggested to the strikers that I felt that my fellow directors were unable to handle the situation, when I knew they were perfectly capable of doing so.

I got back to Cobbold Road on the very day that Roy Grantham was addressing the annual conference of the TUC on the Grunwick dispute. This was the notorious speech in which he described me as 'a reactionary employer taking advantage of race'. If he had known the colour of my skin, I doubt whether Mr Grantham would have made this racialist slur. I would have sued him for defamation, but for the fact that one of the many legal immunities enjoyed by our trade union leaders is, I am advised, immunity from being sued for libel in the course of a trade dispute.

I found that left-wing militants, using the APEX umbrella, moved in to take control of the strike. In the months that followed, it often seemed to us that APEX was being used to provide a cover of respectability for extremist elements. The pickets were now organised by a new body calling itself the Grunwick Strike Committee. Its chairman Nuraly Valiani was a Pakistani who had only been with Grunwick for a short time and had been sacked from his previous job. Its secretary, Mahmood Ahmed, had worked for us for precisely two weeks, and never did an hour's overtime in the period he worked for us, but had been deducted time for lateness. However, he soon displayed his skills as a propagandist by disseminating stories like the famous claim that at Grunwick you have to put your hand up to go to the lavatory. The treasurer of this Strike Committee was Mrs Desai, soon to become the heroine of countless strike posters.

But the moving spirit behind the committee was undoubtedly Jack Dromey. During the Scarman hearings, Dromey and Tom Durkin, the Chairman of the Brent Trades Council, both referred to the pickets as being like 'chickens out of a coop' before they moved in to tell them what to do. This is an appropriate moment to say something about the role of a young activist who probably did more than anyone else to escalate a small dispute at a small company into a confrontation between union might and the rule of law.

Jack Dromey was prepared to accept a description of himself as an 'agitator' during the Scarman hearings. He became a familiar figure outside the factory gates, a heavily-built man with a bushy beard, habitually clad in a black leather jacket. Our workers, who are quick to give a nickname to most people soon took to calling Dromey 'Jackboot'.

By the time he involved himself at Grunwick, Dromey was already recognised as one of the prime 'stirrers' in the Brent area, which is a political playground for extreme movements, not only those in which Dromey is involved but an odd assortment including squatters' movements, Communists, Trotskyites, the Provisional Sinn Fein and black power groups, and in which council services, community centres and tenants' associations have been colonised by the ultra-left.

Dromey was employed by the Brent Community Law centre, whose shabby office, with no notice board to identify it, is in Church Road, NW 10. The Law Centre survives on £38,320 of public money, of which three-quarters comes from central government funds and the rest from the local rates. Jack Dromey's job as a 'community development officer' with the Law Centre provided a base for his political excursions; he told the Scarman Inquiry that this was possible because of his 'flexible working hours'. One of Dromey's colleagues on the staff of the Law Centre was Pamela Scotcher, the Secretary of the Willesden Branch of the Communist Party.

Dromey also sat on a range of local authorities, such as the Brent and Harrow District Manpower Committee, a sub-committee of the Brent Education Committee, and the local supplementary benefits appeal tribunal.

But Dromey was better known as Secretary of the Brent Trades Council and local delegate to the south-eastern region of the TUC. It was as secretary of the Trades Council that Dromey seized the opportunity to involve himself at Grunwick.

Jack Dromey was a notable figure in left-wing circles before Grunwick. Before our strike began, he was arrested for insulting behaviour during violent demonstrations outside the

Trico works in Western Road, Ealing, and fined £50 at the subsequent Court hearing for this offence. In 1976 he became the National Chairman of the National Council for Civil Liberties; and under NCCL auspices he went to Angola to attend the trial of the British mercenaries there. He afterwards remained on the NCCL's national committee, specialising in Northern Irish affairs. (The NCCL was quick off the mark to complain about alleged police misconduct once the clashes with the mass pickets began outside our factory.)

From his headquarters Dromey organised the lobbying of left-wing Labour MPs, a programme for strangling Grunwick by cutting off vital supplies and services, and the publication of the regular bulletins of the Grunwick Strike Committee. He could count on Parliamentary backing from the word 'go'. Sydney Bidwell, the former Chairman of the Tribune Group, was among the first Labour MPs to take an interest in the Grunwick conflict. Bidwell's political leanings could be gauged from the article he published a year later in a Communist organ, *Morning Star*, in which he said that he differed from the Communist Party on only one major point. Unlike the Communists, Bidwell thought that 'civil war' might be inevitable in order to bring about genuine socialism in Britain.

Two of the MPs in the Brent area also stood on the extreme left of the Labour Party. Reg Freeson, the Minister for Housing, is MP for Brent East. He was the founder of *Searchlight* magazine, which he edited between 1960 and 1962. The publication claims to campaign against the revival of Fascism in Britain. Laurie Pavitt, the MP for Brent South, is a friend of Freeson, and it was he who attacked Grunwick in the House of Commons as a 'sweatshop' with a 'Dickensian' management. Pavitt and Freeson pledged support to Dromey and the Grunwick Strike Committee as early as 14 September 1976.

Under Dromey's supervision the Strike Committee engaged in a fairly professional agitprop campaign. The strike bulletin, issued under the name and logo of APEX, was a prize example of how to practise the technique of the big lie. As late as October 1976 the strike bulletin was still claiming that 200 process workers—not 137—had walked out of Grunwick, and was still claiming that we paid our workers a basic rate of £25 for a thirty-five-hour week, despite the fact that only a minority of trainees had ever received this wage. Dromey later explained to the Scarman inquiry that it is 'normal trade union practice' to quote the lowest figures available in trade disputes, whether or not they are representative.

The earliest issues of this strike bulletin gave us some idea of what we were in for. Number 3, published early in September, swore that 'within seven to ten days, our blacking will ensure that only a trickle of work will get through to the factories ... the blacking will be 80 per cent effective in one week's time. Every time the employer thinks up a new trick we will foil it'. That, of course, was a promise that Jack Dromey and his friends were unable to keep. Tom Durkin threatened in the next issue of the strike bulletin, dated 16 September, that they would bring the company down. 'The management,' he declared, 'does not understand the great power of the trade union movement and its ability to bring Grunwick to its knees.'

Apart from holding endless marches, demonstrations and mass meetings at the Brent Trades and Labour Hall, the Strike Committee was having some success in the early weeks in blacking our supplies, and was putting the squeeze on our remaining workforce in an effort to bring them out to join the picket line. But Dromey's propaganda served to stiffen our resolve, and the exaggerated claims in the strike bulletins about our imminent defeat must have brought rapid disenchantment to those who started by swallowing them whole. The strike committee's wild allegations about slave labour conditions inside the firm only served to offend our workers who knew what the situation was really like.

Still, the strike committee was able to mobilise the union brothers in other firms that we dealt with. Kodak, for example, told us that they were going to black us at a time

when we were spending about £2 million with them every
year. The drivers of British Oxygen refused to make
deliveries. Workers at Heathrow Airport also agreed to black
Grunwick shipments, so we had to stop using this airport for
our export trade. The Post Office drivers stopped making
collections and deliveries by van.

But it did not take us long to learn the arts of blockade-
busting. By one means or another, we managed to get our
supplies through, and found ways to send our shipments
abroad. But we felt very isolated at this early stage. After all,
we were just a small company, subjected to a tremendous
propaganda barrage, sniped at by MPs and union chiefs who
had never set foot inside the firm. Neither I nor my
fellow-directors were absentee directors who could cheerfully
write off the loss if we went down. We had sunk our life
savings and many years of our lives into the company. The
jobs of our workers were not an abstraction to us, since we
had always 'led from the front'. We were determined to
guarantee their livelihoods, whatever the cost.

They were being harassed in their own homes and in the
streets. They were being told that if they did not join the
pickets they would never be able to get a job with any other
firm in the area, and that we would be forced to lick the
union's boots. I was only beginning to learn how fortunate we
were to have people working for us with such tremendous
physical courage. Little Asian girls had the Brent Indian
Workers' Association visiting them at night telling them they
were letting down their community. They had words like
'scab' painted on their doors. Their husbands and families
were pestered by spokesmen for the papers. Some of them
were threatened that they would be beaten up if they refused
to leave their job. Yet most of them held out.

All the fine talk about what trade unionism meant might
have won more respect from us if it had not been associated
in our minds, from the very beginning, with the thuggery that
was practised in its name. What made it all the worse was
that the victims, in many cases, were people who had been

forced out of their former countries under the most harrowing circumstances.

I have already told the story of Azadi Patel. This was one of the worst cases of intimidation, but it was by no means untypical. One of the most respected Asian workers at the Cobbold Road factory, for example, is Arvind Patel. He came to England from Uganda in March 1975. He used to run a highly successful commercial agency, which amongst other things was the agent for the major tyre companies including Michelin. He was one of the many thousands of refugees from Idi Amin. He was forced to flee the country after Amin's toughs arrested several of his friends and looted his store. He had to leave personal assets worth 400,000 shillings in Uganda because he was not allowed to take anything out with him. At forty-one, he is regarded as an uncle by many members of the staff.

Arvind is not a strong man. He is slight and very frail, with a heart condition. he was physically menaced. Arvind has instituted a private prosecution of one of the pickets; at the date this book was written, the proceedings were pending. Several people, who said they were members of the Brent Indian Workers' Association, have put pressure on Arvind's relatives to persuade him to stop working for Grunwick. But he has kept on coming to work every day.

We had a young girl at Cobbold Road called Nalini Chohan, who came over from Nairobi in 1974 and got her first job with us. She had been having trouble with her landlord and it was suggested to her that she might be able to get help to obtain a flat if she was prepared to side with the pickets. Nalini says that the pickets visited her at her home six or seven times, often arriving in the middle of dinner. On one occasion, they threatened that if she went out by herself, she would be beaten up. She is a fiery young thing, and doesn't take that type of threat lying down. She told the pickets that if they had the guts to try to beat her up, they were welcome to try.

7

A little help from my friends

After the first couple of months, it was obvious that the pickets were not going to go away. In mid-October, strike pay was increased from £12 to £18 a week, and the people on the picket lines were also being paid food and travelling expenses. Chemists who sent films to Grunwick were being systematically visited and urged to stop dealing with us. But this was an insignificant threat when compared with the new one that materialised on Friday 29 October when the national executive of the Union of Post Office Workers (UPW) instructed its members not to handle Grunwick mail.

As I said at the time, this was a threat to our jugular. From the very beginning, strikers had been able to count on powerful allies, while the company looked very isolated. Laurie Pavitt, Reg Freeson, and Alderman Hartley, leader of the Brent Council, had all been telling us that we were responsible for major disruption in the area and that we should recognise the union and take the strikers back. It was my wife, Loretto, who suggested that it was high time that we set out to find some political support of our own. We arranged through a friend who was active in the local Conservative party, to meet John Gorst, my MP for Hendon North, and John Hickey and I went along to see him at the House of Commons. We told him about the threatened postal blacking, and how this could destroy our business, since 84 per cent of our trade depended on mail order. He expressed his sympathy, but we left the House feeling that there was not much that we could do.

When I came into the office the following Monday, 1 November, I found Malcolm Alden and John Hickey looking very glum. They told me that the postal sorters at WC1 had refused to handle our mail. I asked them what they had done about it, and they said 'nothing'. I told them that they should immediately get the Post Office to explain their action in writing. I phoned our solicitors, and they confirmed that it appeared there was very little we could do, as they had already carefully reviewed this matter with Counsel, who had advised that, although the law was on our side, in practice legal action would probably prove ineffective.

Fortunately, the evening before I had heard a programme on BBC4 on the closed shop. The man who was leading the debate against compulsory unionisation was a Roger Webster, who had been sacked some time before by British Rail for refusing to join a union under a closed shop agreement. He argued with spirit, but also with a dry humour that impressed me. I found myself in total agreement with the thoughts that he expressed.

He was described on the radio as the National Branch Organiser for the National Association for Freedom, a body which had been branded by the left as extreme right-wing. I certainly did not intend to get involved in any extremist organisation. My position is a simple one: there are certain principles of individual liberty on which I am prepared to take a stand; and if any honest and reputable organisation offers me help in the battle that follows I will accept it gladly. But it is that way round, not the other. I will work with an organisation in pursuit of particular ends that seem to me important: I have not and I never will take any line of action because it fits in with the policy of some political body. If the Labour Party had been truly concerned with the rights of workers and had been willing to help Grunwick stand out against those who sought to deprive them of those rights, I would have accepted their help as happily as that of NAFF or the Conservative Party.

After hearing Roger Webster talk I decided to get in touch with NAFF. The first piece of help I got from them was practical and important. They recommended solicitors who after consulting Counsel advised me that legal action would prove effective. They pointed out that to interfere with the collection and delivery of the Royal Mail is a criminal offence under the Post Office Act of 1953. They suggested that we should apply at once for an injunction to stop the blacking, and we promptly applied for injunctive relief to the High Court.

Meanwhile, the postal blacking had been going on for four days, and the loyalty of the workforce was being stretched to the limit. The pickets were cheering every Post Office van that passed our gates.

But relief was in sight. As our solicitors pushed ahead with the High Court application, John Gorst arranged an emergency debate in the House of Commons, and it at once became clear that opinion was beginning to rally to our side. The combination of the two forms of pressure weakened the resolve of Tom Jackson, the leader of the UPW. He called off the blacking, and it was announced at the time that the reason was that Grunwick had agreed to cooperate with the official arbitration service, ACAS. As the Scarman report conceded later, this statement by Mr Albert Booth, the Secretary for Employment, misrepresented the facts. The UPW blacking was called off on 4 November because of the combined effect of the threat of legal action and Parliamentary pressure. When the case was finally heard in the High Court Mr Jackson gave a solemn undertaking that the blacking would not be repeated.

During the postal boycott I had spoken to our management. I said I was unsure as to how long it would take to raise the boycott and that it was possible that the company would have to go into liquidation. Without dissent, everyone agreed that it would be preferable to liquidate rather than capitulate to a Trade Union which was endeavouring, against the wishes of our workforce, to bludgeon its way by brute force into our company. The ending of the four-day postal boycott was the first real blow that the strike organisers had suffered. It was a blow to their morale and a tremendous boost to the morale of our staff.

John Hickey and I attended the emergency debate, which we were able to watch from the VIP section of the Visitors' Gallery. Roy Grantham and Tom Jackson were sitting in the same row. I had been warned by John Gorst that the Conservatives would stick to the law and order issue, and that the Labour Party, since it was on such weak ground here, would probably set out to throw as much muck at the company as possible in order to confuse basic issues. Albert Booth, and his deputy, Harold Walker, fielded most of the questions for the government. Surprisingly, Sam Silkin, the Attorney General—and the man who refused to apply the criminal law throughout the Grunwick dispute—did not bother to attend. On the Labour side, Laurie Pavitt got up and rehearsed his line about how Grunwick had sprung straight from the Dickensian era, how the staff had to put up their hands to go to the lavatory, and how starvation wages were paid. Mrs Audrey Wise came in after the debate was under way and got up to say that 'these workers are being treated more like slaves.' She left the Chamber after a few minutes. This comment by this left-wing MP gave rise to a *Daily Mirror* headline 'Inside the Factory of Slaves'—incidentally by a reporter who had not visited our factory. Mrs Wise was subsequently arrested for alleged obstruction while participating in a mass picket outside our premises in June.

It was clear from that debate that few Conservatives, up to this point, had taken a detailed interest in the Grunwick affair. They were not as well briefed as the left-wingers. I think that they were inhibited by the failure of their attempts to resist the miners' demands in 1974, when Mr Heath twice attempted to do so and was twice forced to admit defeat. This certainly produced in some Conservatives a belief that it was necessary to compromise with the unions, even over basic matters of principle, that Britain cannot be governed against their wishes, and that the law cannot be invoked in trade disputes.

I have no wish to become involved in debates within the Conservative Party. I believe that those on both sides are moved by honourable motives and one can certainly see why they hold the beliefs they do. But it must be obvious that I do not personally accept that compromise will help the problem to go away, and in the situation that Grunwick faced at this time any talk of compromise on our part was totally unrealistic. However flexible a character I may be myself, the choice had been taken away from us by our opponents. If we had given in under union pressure and reinstated the strikers, we would have aroused such anger and resentment in the workers who had stood by us that the factory would have become unmanageable. We could choose between the risk of a quick death and the certainty of a slow one. In that position, what compromise is possible?

We did, however, agree to let Roy Grantham come to Grunwick to see conditions for himself and to talk to the workforce. This actually happened in the following June, though in a rather curious way. Grantham came to the gate at Chapter Road, claiming that the mass picketing had forced us to talk to him. In fact, I had issued an invitation to him to talk not to me, but to our staff. John Gouriet, the Administrative Director of NAFF, was there to chair the meeting, much to Grantham's annoyance.

When he got inside the mail order section he got up on the table and began by saying to the staff 'We want an end to the problem—we want a just solution. We want our members reinstated and our union recognised'. But all the people he wanted reinstated had been abusing and cursing the staff for months before, and our workers reacted in a way that would have been entirely predictable to anyone who had considered it. They had before them the man they regarded as responsible for the picketing and harassment they had had to endure. And instead of apologising for what they had suffered, he was arrogantly imposing conditions. They howled him down. He later alleged that they had been primed with drink, but no one had been drinking over there—we don't serve alcohol in the canteen, and during the mass pickets our workers have felt unable to go to local pubs where they would be likely to meet rent-a-mob people from outside the gates.

The background to this meeting in any case entirely disproves Grantham's story about the drink. I had left Chapter Road to go to the Cobbold Road plant with John

Gouriet that day, and we were round there after lunch. We were then told that Grantham was at Chapter Road seeking to talk to me. I initially refused to have this meeting, since I had consistently declined to have an individual meeting with him, because I knew the staff would be extremely upset if they felt that I was arranging any kind of a private deal with him. But I agreed to set up a meeting with the staff at 2.45. Gouriet went over to meet Grantham. What was said between them I don't know, but the meeting was to enable Grantham to meet the staff, not me. It took place at 4.00 p.m. I was present.

I told the staff to listen to Grantham and see what he wanted of them. As I was saying this, someone yelled from the floor, 'Yes, Mr Ward, but he hasn't given us a chance to say what we think'. It was clear that I was beginning to get somewhat unpopular with my workers for even suggesting that the union leader should have an uninterrupted say. When they started baying for his blood, he began searching for a scapegoat, and blamed Gouriet, who was chairing the meeting.

Grantham's account of what took place can be compared with the film that was taken by the BBC cameramen who were present. The film footage shows several things clearly. It shows Grantham patting Gouriet on the head in an attempt to belittle him. It shows the anger of my workers. What it does not show is what Grantham said to Tom Hambrook, a member of our Works Committee, who asked him whether he would like to attend one of its meetings. Grantham told Tom, 'I don't talk to office boys.' Nothing, I think, could so clearly demonstrate the arrogance of so many of those who claim to be speaking for the ordinary worker.

8

What about the workers?

The word uncompromising is rarely used as a term of praise. Since the beginning of the Grunwick dispute, I have frequently been called 'uncompromising'. Roy Grantham and others have said that it is because I am uncompromising that the union movement has been 'compelled' to contemplate extreme measures like mass picketing, and the illegal boycott of services to my company. But it is not always easy to compromise, nor desirable. Letting Hitler have the Sudetenland was a compromise; so was letting him have the whole of Czechoslovakia later on.

Many people will think this analogy far-fetched. But I have never believed that it is possible, or desirable, to split the difference where principles are involved. I tried to act throughout the Grunwick dispute in accordance with the law of the land and the wishes of our workforce. I saw no reason to accept half of what APEX was trying to impose on our company, especially since I saw little reason why APEX should have involved itself in the first place. Mr Grantham said many times that his union had sought to offer us 'a way out': through the appointment of an 'impartial' mediator by the government, through a court of inquiry whose recommendations would be accepted as mandatory, through the official arbitration service, ACAS. Our reluctance to accept any of these courses led Mr Grantham to explain, in the course of the Scarman hearings, that 'we were dealing with a most unusual employer—a very hard, or, as I would call it, a very reactionary employer—who was determined to have his own way'. He added: 'In my experience as a senior trade union official and indeed throughout my working life as a trade unionist, I have never come across a company which has been so averse to the normal procedures of conciliation and negotiation as Grunwick.'

If that is a fair comment, I suspect that it reflects the acquiescence of many larger companies than Grunwick in the corporate order that trade union power has been seeking to impose in Britain. I might have had more confidence in the forms of arbitration and 'conciliation' that were offered if it had been possible to believe in their full impartiality.

The Advisory Conciliation and Arbitration Service (ACAS) appeared on the scene very early on. Within a week of the walk out, it had offered its services as a mediator. It made further advances during September, which the company declined. If I had known more about ACAS and the details of the 1975 Employment Protection Act under which it was set up at the beginning of the dispute, I would have been even less enthusiastic.

The 1975 Act implicitly gave ACAS the statutory duty of introducing trade unionism to non-unionised companies. The very first section of the act observed that 'The Service shall be charged with the duty of encouraging the extension of collective bargaining'—which means trade unions. It would seem that ACAS is prevented under the law from acting truly impartially in conflicts between the unions and employers. Indeed, a leading business consultant, Robert Fleeman has observed that 'an ACAS man who claims to be acting impartially in such matters should be dropped like a hot potato; he is either disregarding his duty or he is intentionally deceiving you.'

ACAS is a statutory body set up by the Employment Protection Act 1975. It includes representatives of employers, trade unions and others. It is independent of the government although its Council is appointed by the Secretary of State for Employment. Any trade union can lodge a claim with ACAS against an employer demanding that he should recognise it for the purpose of collective bargaining. ACAS is required under the 1975 Act to try to settle such a claim by conciliation. If this fails, it is empowered to hold consultations and make inquiries. At the end of the day, it has a wider power: it can recommend that an employer should grant recognition to a union. If the employer still refuses to recognise a union, the union can then take him before a superior body called the Central Arbitration Committee. The trade union can present its demands for wage increases or other improvements in working conditions to this committee, which has the power to make awards in accordance with such demands. If these awards are made, these terms become part of the contract of service for each employee in the company. So in this roundabout way, the union can seek to determine the conditions at a company where the employer (and perhaps his workforce) are opposed to union recognition; it remains doubtful under the existing law whether an employer can actually be compelled legally to give formal recognition to the union all the same.

The Chairman of ACAS, Jim Mortimer, was quoted in the *Guardian* on 30 June as saying: 'My understanding is that Parliament intends ACAS to promote collective bargaining based on trade union recognition as the best method of conducting industrial relations.' How can a body with this *raison d'être* be regarded as independent in judging the question of union recognition? It was created, after all, as part of the danegeld that the Labour government paid to the union leaders.

But without having studied the background to ACAS, we had a perfectly straightforward reason for declining its original overtures. We thought there was very little that the arbitration service could do to help us reach a settlement because the conflict revolved around the sacking of the strikers, and we had received the legal advice that we had either to dismiss the lot or to take them all back—which we were not prepared to do.

Mr Grantham had a rather different view of the matter. On 15 October APEX referred its claim for recognition to ACAS, as it was entitled to do under Section 11 of the 1975 Act. We met with ACAS representatives on 26 October, and said that we were willing to cooperate—which made a nonsense of Albert Booth's later claim that the November postal boycott was called off because we felt obliged to cooperate with ACAS later on. I remember meeting Harry Bainbridge, the Director of the South East region of ACAS, who explained the rules of the game to me. It seemed to me that the rules were made up as you went along and you didn't know who was scoring the goals. I asked, for example, whether, if the majority of our workforce did not wish to recognise a union, ACAS would respect their views in making its recommendations. I said we would be ready to work on that basis. But ACAS would not give any undertaking—it seemed that there were no rules.

Our view throughout was that the proper subject for any ACAS enquiry was the opinion of our workers. ACAS insisted that it must take account of the views of the people who had been dismissed. We also had differences over the way that a ballot should be conducted inside the firm. ACAS wished to conduct a ballot department by department, which would have meant that, if, for example, there was a majority vote of one in one of our departments in favour of union recognition, while everybody else voted against it, ACAS might well feel free to recommend union recognition for that one department. What annoyed me most was the assumption that some official arbitrator could walk into a company to which we had given our blood, sweat, toil and tears and tell us precisely what to do, as if he had some God-given insight that we lacked. This rankled with me, since I have always been a person who believes in pursuing his business with the minimum of government assistance or interference.

Once again, we turned to the lawyers. ACAS insisted that the pickets should be balloted. It maintained that they were workers to whom the issue related. I could not understand how this could be so, since I had sacked them and had no intention of ever re-employing them. I was puzzled about other things too. ACAS said that it was going to get our workers to fill in a questionnaire which, in our view, meant a ballot, but which they said was an 'enquiry'.

This distinction between a ballot and an enquiry may seem a very fine one but in fact it is important in the context of the

Employment Protection Act. If what is being conducted is a ballot, the employer has certain rights to make his own representations to ACAS, which must then take them into account. With an enquiry he has no such rights.

We were advised that what ACAS proposed to hold would, within the meaning of the Act, be a ballot, and they could not explain to us why they considered it to be an enquiry, which as we saw it would deprive us of the rights we should have had. Our lawyers supported the view that, in these circumstances, we should not give ACAS the names and addresses of our workers. We were never opposed to the viewpoints of our workers being tested, and later held two independent opinion polls. But we did dig in our heels when it came to considering the views of our former employees in dispute. Our legal advisers supported our decision not to provide access to our current employees as long as there were important issues to be resolved between us. Discussions went on right up until Christmas time. We were finally notified in a letter from ACAS on 20 December that they intended to go ahead and send their questionnaire to the strikers.

In February ACAS produced a draft report; on 10 March it formally recommended that Grunwick should recognise APEX. Its ballot of the strikers, who were no longer our employees, had unsurprisingly produced an overwhelming majority in favour of union recognition.

We were staggered by the idea that any recommendation could be issued that was not in accord with the views of our own workers. We challenged the legality of the ACAS report, and the Lord Chief Justice, Lord Widgery, found in favour of the defendants, ACAS and APEX, in the High Court on 12 July. Two weeks later Lord Denning, in the Court of Appeal, found in our favour.

Lord Denning based his judgement on the definition of 'workers to whom the issue relates'. He maintained that when ACAS held a formal ballot (as even the High Court had conceded that it had) the ballot should take account of the views of all the workers to whom the issue related, and not merely some of them, or those which ACAS considered fit.

ACAS sent round papers with questions expressed in both English and Gujerati. Recipients would be told that their answers would be strictly confidential. ACAS reported 91 votes in favour of union recognition, one 'Don't know' and one 'No'. Both Lord Widgery and Lord Denning agreed that although ACAS defined this as a questionnaire, it amounted to a formal ballot. As Lord Denning put it, ACAS made 'a fatal mistake' by not sending their ballot papers to any of our weekly paid staff. The workers in our factory were left unheard.

The legal battle did not, of course, end there. ACAS and APEX were given leave to appeal to the House of Lords, where, as I completed this book, the matter was waiting for a hearing in November. Grunwick's position was always clear. We always maintained that we would abide by the law of the land, but would refuse to bow to pressure from outside the courts.

We were widely criticised for not giving the names and addresses of our employees to ACAS. I hardly think that it would have been reasonable to do so, since we were given no guidance on whether ACAS would be in any way bound by their opinions. As we understood the matter, ACAS would be free to recommend union recognition even if 90 per cent of our employees voted against it. We have been equally widely criticised for allegedly dragging our heels in dealings with ACAS. The easiest reply to that is the fact that the ACAS report on Grunwick was issued less than six months after our dispute had been referred to the service by APEX. This compares with an average gap of nine and a half months between reference and the issuing of a report in other companies in which ACAS became involved in 1976. (There were some delays as long as thirteen months.)

In refusing to assist ACAS in distributing its 'questionnaire' we had no intention of gagging our employees. We demonstrated this by organising two independent opinion polls. The first was conducted by the Market and Opinion Research International (MORI) organisation, a highly respected body which has done work for the Labour Party. It polled the workforce on 25 February. The MORI poll showed that 86 per cent of those questioned did not wish to have a union to negotiate for them. It was alleged by my critics that I had instructed my staff to give 'a big no' to the union. It was completely untrue that I issued any such instructions, or sought to apply any improper pressures. Significantly, the MORI poll also showed that precisely 2 members of the staff wanted APEX to be recognised. Out of a total of 21 who said they were in favour of trade union recognition, no fewer than 16 said that they did not know what union they wanted, and another 2 said 'any' union would do.

We held another opinion poll on 20 July. This one was conducted by Gallup, and it produced equally impressive results. Only 6 per cent of those questioned said that they wanted a trade union to negotiate for them. 85 per cent were opposed to union recognition, and 87 per cent said they did not wish to be members of APEX. (Only 3 per cent said that they wished to be APEX members.) 82 per cent said that they were opposed to reinstatement of the strikers who had been sacked. The Scarman report concluded that 'there is no evidence that Mr Ward exerted pressure on his workforce in respect of this poll'. It confirmed what we had known all along: that the Grunwick workforce was united in its desire neither to have a union at the company nor to see the strikers reinstated.

9

Life among the pickets

According to the first strike bulletin put out by the Strike Committee in 1977, this was going to be the year when the 'sweat-shop' would be closed down. The main technique to be used was mass picketing. Analogies were drawn with what had happened at the Saltley Coke Depot in 1972, when the then Home Secretary, Reginald Maudling, had withdrawn the police in the face of large-scale picketing. If it could happen at Saltley under a Conservative government, why shouldn't it happen at Grunwick under a Labour government?

According to Jack Dromey, it was 'romantic passion' that kept the pickets outside our gates through the long winter, and into the summer of 1977, when 'romantic passion' again brought workers flocking to Willesden from all over the country to join a mass picket. It is worth observing that the Grunwick pickets were paid £34 or more per week for their romantic passion by the summer of 1977. APEX raised its strike pay from an initial £8 a week to £34 and this was supplemented, in most cases, by additional payments by the Grunwick Strike Committee. APEX was not short of cash; Grantham declared on 17 June that his union had £2 million in assets, and had put £300,000 into the bank in the previous year. APEX, like other major unions, was raking in a large tax-free income through increased members' subscriptions, which provided a ready cash reserve to finance activities that the rank and file membership may well have opposed. It should not be forgotten that the bulk of union income is tax-free because unions are classified as provident societies, which would leave one to imagine that they spend a substantial proportion of their residue on members' benefits. In fact, the proportion spent on members' benefits is derisory; and the overwhelming bulk of union income goes on administration.

Was it again 'romantic passion' that brought trade unionists from up and down the country to Dollis Hill to back the Grunwick pickets after 13 June, when mass picketing began? The miners were paid £15 a day plus £5 for expenses in London plus travelling expenses. A nice, economical way to have a day out in London. Many of the young militants mobilised by the extreme left groups were unemployed people on the dole and on supplementary benefits.

This is a convenient point to deal with the allegation that I 'bribed' my workers to keep coming to work, in breach of the government's pay policy. The 'bribery' was going on at the picket lines, not inside Grunwick. Some of our workers were even offered housing as an inducement to join the strike. At least one *part-time* worker was able to 'earn' more from strike pay—which was increased by several hundred per cent in the course of the strike—than she had taken home before.

It is true that we gave pay increases after the strike began. But they were no bigger in percentage terms than in previous years, and one excellent reason for giving them, in addition to the workers' proven loyalty, was that productivity had improved by up to fifty per cent since the trouble-makers left. This has meant that over the last eighteen months, despite good increases in wages, we have not had to raise our prices to the public.

The relevant figures for wage increases at Grunwick are as follows:

April 1974	8–15%
June 1974	16% across the board
April 1975	11–18%
April 1976	5–13%
November 1976	15% across the board
April 1977	10% across the board

Someone described the scenes outside Grunwick that summer as 'the Ascot of the left': everyone who was *anyone* on the left in Britain had to be seen there, bellowing through a megaphone, vying with his rivals in revolutionary rhetoric.

9

Life among the pickets

According to the first strike bulletin put out by the Strike Committee in 1977, this was going to be the year when the 'sweat-shop' would be closed down. The main technique to be used was mass picketing. Analogies were drawn with what had happened at the Saltley Coke Depot in 1972, when the then Home Secretary, Reginald Maudling, had withdrawn the police in the face of large-scale picketing. If it could happen at Saltley under a Conservative government, why shouldn't it happen at Grunwick under a Labour government?

According to Jack Dromey, it was 'romantic passion' that kept the pickets outside our gates through the long winter, and into the summer of 1977, when 'romantic passion' again brought workers flocking to Willesden from all over the country to join a mass picket. It is worth observing that the Grunwick pickets were paid £34 or more per week for their romantic passion by the summer of 1977. APEX raised its strike pay from an initial £8 a week to £34 and this was supplemented, in most cases, by additional payments by the Grunwick Strike Committee. APEX was not short of cash; Grantham declared on 17 June that his union had £2 million in assets, and had put £300,000 into the bank in the previous year. APEX, like other major unions, was raking in a large tax-free income through increased members' subscriptions, which provided a ready cash reserve to finance activities that the rank and file membership may well have opposed. It should not be forgotten that the bulk of union income is tax-free because unions are classified as provident societies, which would leave one to imagine that they spend a substantial proportion of their revenue on members' benefits. In fact, gates, moving through the gap in the picket lines that the police were struggling to keep open, toughs would surge forward in an effort to get to him; there would be three or four more arrests required in order to get a single worker through to the plant. That mob in the street was not trying to coax our workforce: it was snarling insults and threats at them.

Watching all this from my window, I realised that the dispute had acquired a new dimension. Some of the staff came very close to violence that day. We had said we would send out a minibus to pick up workers from outlying stations if they could not get through the gates on foot. In fact, we were unable to get the minibus out that morning. We had been fortunate that the workers who stayed with us were fighters, but it was clearly too much to expect frail Asian girls to brave the bully boys day after day. I saw Jessie Patel, one of our Asian supervisors, struggling to get through with her bad leg.

It was a bad morning. My confidence was shaken. By the end of the day, eighty-four people had been arrested for obstruction and assault, and Grantham, the moderate, was claiming that 'the people here are picketing peacefully'. A very few members of our staff had turned back at the sight of the picket line, and we had to send cars to fetch them later on and bring them round to the back of the factory. It was obvious that we could not expect the workers to go on day after day facing this kind of intimidation.

Malcolm Alden solved the problem by getting hold of an old school bus. Malcolm had learnt from a friend that you could drive a bus on a private licence as long as you owned it and did not charge any fares. I was a bit sceptical to begin with about buying a bus, but Malcolm remembered that his son had gone to his school camp a couple of weeks before, when the teacher's brother had driven a red single-decker bus. Malcolm sent his wife round to the school to find out about it. They let us borrow it for a while, which enabled us to drive it on a private licence; you are not allowed to do this if you actually hire a bus.

We at once drew up a list of pick-up points. The red bus took the staff out of the factory that day; and they were told where they would be able to board it the following morning. For the first week or so, Malcolm drove the workers into Chapter Road on the red bus.

The Socialist Workers' Party claimed that more than half the pickets arested on the first day of mass picketing were their members. Yet in his statement the following day, Mr Grantham, while accusing the police of 'provocation' and 'brutality', did not complain of the role of this party which is openly committed to armed revolution in Britain and whose paper, *Socialist Worker*, has condoned violence against the police. There was a similar ambiguity in the relations between the 'moderate' trade unionists and the bovver boys throughout the picketing. From time to time the 'moderates' would verbally dissociate themselves from the thug element; yet in the next breath they would blame the violence on the police or the intransigence of the company.

The numbers of flying pickets built up in the following days. On 17 June 1500 pickets converged on Grunwick. That day, the pickets tried to let down the tyres of the bus, and threw missiles and tin cans at its windows. One policeman's ankle was broken, and the pickets around him shouted 'Hope the bastard dies' and 'One down, another five hundred to go' as he was taken off in an ambulance. One picket pulled a knife on the police.

Obviously embarrassed, Roy Grantham called for a limit of five hundred pickets two days later 'for the sake of peace'. But APEX seemed less than fully committed to cooling it on the picket lines, since Chris Wright, another top APEX official, declared the very next day at the Strike Committee's HQ that 'We hope to get five thousand in the streets ... so that we can get this factory closed'.

The mob had plenty of others to egg them on. That same day, Eric Heffer, the Tribunite MP, attacked the company and declared that 'if six hundred policemen were mobilised to allow these strike breakers to go to work, it is perfectly understandable that responsible trade unionists from every trade union in the country should show their solidarity'. This, in our view, was incitement to violence in order to coerce 'strike breakers'—regardless of whether the strike itself is justified. Heffer's appeal for trade unionists to come from all over the country had already been heard. The day after he spoke, Dennis MacShane, the vice-president of the National Union of Journalists, was one of those arrested on the picket line. The participation of an NUJ leader was significant in view of that union's determined attempt to impose the closed shop on journalists throughout the country.

Roy Grantham rehearsed the propaganda theme favoured by the Trotskyites, that the troublemakers on the picket lines were plain clothes men or 'outsiders' (by implication, policemen) who threw milk bottles in an effort to discredit the trade unions involved.

McGahey and Arthur Scargill, the Yorkshire miners' president, declared their intention of joining the picket on 23 June. McGahey declared 'We certainly hope we will do a Saltley—close the place up and stop that industrial hooligan Mr Ward in his tracks.' Scargill gathered his cohorts to march south. He announced 'We will bring down thousands of miners from the whole of the membership of our union. We will not allow the trade union movement to be defeated.'

It was a day of savage violence. It was the day when PC Trevor Wilson had his head cut open by a milk bottle, while left-wing pickets howled 'Kill the bastard'. In all, thirteen people were injured. The police arrested fifty pickets, including Arthur Scargill. One of his aides, Percy Reilly, warned 'The police will rue the day they arrested Arthur'.

But a man like 'King Arthur' is not stopped by a single arrest. Scargill bobbed up again the following day, calling for a 'day of national protest' on 11 July, and for 25,000 trade unionists to picket Grunwick. Not everyone in the NUM took the same line. Len Clark, the chief of the miners in Nottinghamshire, said the same day that he would refuse to allow official NUM pickets to join the mob outside Grunwick, and that to pay miners to go down would be a misuse of union funds. He was outflanked by one of his local militants, however—Joseph Whelan, the financial secretary—who urged local NUM members to go down, and said that he would go down himself. In the face of such threats, we received eloquent support from Sir Keith Joseph, who summed up the views of the average television viewer in Britain: 'Those faces contorted with hatred, those foul mouths, those ever-ready fists and discordant voices baying for blood like hounds make a mockery of the socialist's claim to be working for human brotherhood. They are the agents of hate and destruction. The battle of Grunwick sorts out the democrats on the one hand from the red fascists and time-servers on the other.'

A few days later, Lord Denning lent his voice to the attack on the incipient anarchy in the streets of north London. 'Our laws,' said Lord Denning, 'are being disregarded right and left. The mobs are out. The police are being subjected to violence. I take no part in the rights or wrongs of these disputes, but I do know that intimidation and violence are contrary to the law of the land'.

The picketing went on and on, and we were visited by more and more of the figureheads of the left. Many Tribunite MPs turned up at one stage or another, and Mrs Audrey Wise was arrested for obstruction. On 4 July Hugh Scanlon dropped in to visit us with eleven members of his executive of the AUEW, including Ken Gill, the Communist general secretary of TASS, the white-collar section of the union. Pickets were brought in by most major unions: the executive council of the National Union of Public Employees (NUPE) called on all its divisions to support the mass picket; the print workers' unions and the NUJ were particularly vociferous; and of course we had the Socialist Workers' Party, the Communist Party and all their rivals on the ultra left vying with each other to show how many bodies they could produce at Dollis Hill.

Despite the massed battalions, we got the Grunwick buses through every day. That is a story in itself, which is told in the next chapter. The alienation of public opinion from those who claimed to be striking in support of the right to join a union outside Grunwick became stronger as the rent-a-mob became more violent, and the actions of some of its leaders more bizarre.

Similarly, the pronouncement of the Marxist group showed that far more was involved at Grunwick, from their viewpoint, than the rights of the workers. *Socialist Worker* was one of the more explicit. 'The events at Grunwick', the paper editorialised on 2 July, 'proved that there is no Parliamentary road to socialism'. The editor of *Socialist Worker*, Paul Foot, speaking at Watford later that month, declared that peaceful picketing was useless at Grunwick. The only way the battle would be won would be through blacking of vital services.

The involvement of the Communists—orthodox and heterodox—was predictable. What depressed me was the help that was given to the strikers by religious and charitable groups who should have known better. The donation of £150 by War on Want, a charity, was only one example. A Methodist minister was present on the picket lines throughout much of the dispute, and earned a stern rebuke in the pages of the *Methodist Recorder*.

As a Catholic, I found that the ambiguous line taken by members of my own Church and by some Catholic papers caused me the greatest concern. The coverage of the Grunwick dispute in the Catholic press seemed to be largely founded on ignorance. The *Catholic Herald* ran an article by a Labour MP, Kevin MacNamara, drawing an absurd analogy between Grunwick and the racial discrimination allegedly practised by British companies in South Africa. I succeeded in having a lengthy reply published. Something similar happened in the case of an editorial in the *Month* whose editor, Hugh Kay, was highly critical of the company, regurgitating the standard left-wing smears; but when I raised the issue with him and demanded to know why he had not checked his facts, he could give me no answer. He knew nothing of the Employment Protection Act, but he went so far as to say that he was on his knees praying to God that the House of Lords would reverse the judgement of the Court of

Appeal, without having ascertained the facts. I said to him that my feeling was that the Christian press should follow the advice of St Thomas Aquinas, who said 'Ask not who is saying the truth, rather ask if the truth is being said'.

10

The Grunwick bus

You don't become a bus driver overnight, least of all when you are faced by an angry mob. On the Wednesday of the first week of the mass picketing, Malcolm drove round the back, down Cooper Road, but was turned back by the police. So he tried to get in the front way, which was also blocked. He found it almost impossible to manouevre, and hit a car. It took a third try before he could get the bus through. That day, we realised that we would need the bus for much more than a week, so Malcolm contacted the school to see if we could buy it. They said it belonged to the Parents and Teachers Association. We knew it was worth about £600, so we offered them double that amount, and they took it.

After the first week of the mass pickets, Malcolm and Ken Pearson asked for permission to buy a second bus, on the grounds that we would be in a very exposed position if the red bus broke down. I told them to go ahead, and they found two splendid blue double-decker buses. They were able to buy them for less than £2,000. The advantage of the double-deckers was that the workers inside were further away from the pickets who were trying to bash at the windows. In the red bus, they were down close to the ground and felt far more vulnerable, even though the windows were fairly small. I suppose that if the pickets had known what little experience the drivers had, they would not have been quite so keen to get in their way. They seemed to believe that we were using professional drivers, from the appeals that they shouted out to Malcolm, and later Ken who drove one of the blue buses, to join the picket lines.

We got the blue buses just in time, since the day that they were ready to go on the road, the axle shaft on the red bus broke. I was watching from my office window that first

Tuesday morning when we brought the blue buses into action. It was very funny. Jack Dromey was standing there with his megaphone outside the gates. A lookout ran up to him to tell him there was a blue bus in the High Street. 'Don't worry, it's nothing to do with us', he said. Then the lookout ran back to say 'Jack, the bus is coming down Chapter Road,' Jack Dromey was still not interested. 'Nothing to do with us.' All at once, our blue bus was coming through the front gate and it was too late for the pickets to make any real demonstration. That incident was quite revealing. Dromey, as the prime stirrer in the conflict, continually under-estimated our determination to resist and our resourcefulness. We were able to outmanoeuvre him at every turn.

The picture of the blue buses going through the picket line has since become familiar to most people in the British Isles and to many people in other countries. The buses would do a tour of the Brent area, picking up workers in two shifts from pre-arranged pick-up points. Since the pickets did not know where these pick-up points were, or where the buses were hidden, there was no harassment at this stage. Trouble would start as the buses approached the factory. The pickets would then surge forward in a concerted attempt to stop the bus, and the main pressure point was always towards the back wheels. We often saw pickets trying to push the policemen under those wheels.

It seems almost miraculous that no one was actually run down by one of the buses. This in itself is a tribute to the driving skill of Ken Pearson and Malcolm Alden, as well as to the courage and efficiency of the police. Ken says that the worst trip he remembers was down Cooper Road, when he had to inch one of the blue buses through a crowd of pickets, literally pushing against policemen who in turn were trying to push the pickets back, and having to stop the bus every few seconds. Two men from the Special Patrol Group were pushed right up against the radiator. They kept saying to Ken, 'Come forward'. Ken was worried that they would be injured if he kept on. One of them insisted, 'Don't worry about us, just push, it's the only way we'll get you through'.

Reluctantly, Ken obeyed. He could see that their arms were being burnt since the radiator was very hot. When he saw them later on that day, after the bus had got through, he asked if they were all right. He says that they were not at all concerned about themselves, just concerned to see that we got through. It was one of many examples of the quiet heroism of the police throughout the Grunwick conflict.

At 5 a.m. on Monday 11 July 1977, I woke up on a camp bed in the office building at Chapter Road. I had slept at the plant overnight, together with four of the managers and a television crew that had come to film the day of the big picket.

I lit up the first cigarette of the day—by this time I was smoking up to sixty a day—and sat down to a breakfast of hot chocolate made with sour milk, with Ken Pearson and Simon Dring, the television reporter. Then we walked to the back of the plant and Ken and I got into a car in order to go and pick up the buses for the workers. The television crew wanted to film us leaving the company premises. This became quite hairy, since pickets were already climbing out of buses at the end of Cooper Road, behind the plant, and advancing down the street. The police were not there in force at that time of the morning and John Hickey was anxious to get us out and close the back gates. We were unable to wait for the cameraman to film this scene as the pickets were now ominously advancing towards the back entrance of the factory at Cooper Road. Ken and I just managed to evade them.

We drove off to where the three Grunwick buses were concealed, and drove all three of them—the two big blue double-deckers and the beaten up red single-decker that we had had from the beginning—off on a zigzag tour of north-west London to kill time until our workers had gathered at the arranged meeting point. We stopped at a workers' cafe for a real breakfast, and then went to a shop owned by a Ugandan Asian to buy cigarettes. I was recognised at this point, and we had to move on hurriedly. Our real concern, as we talked and joked, was whether most of our workers would actually turn up in the face of the threats that had been made. All of them must have been listening to the early morning reports on LBC that had been the start of every morning in my life since the mass picketing began in early June. 'And the pickets are gathering outside Grunwick', LBC's early morning newscaster would rumble. To me it sounded like a call to arms.

When the time came to do the rounds, we got on the buses and wished each other good luck. I went on the bus with Ken Pearson, one of the young Grunwick directors who had become an intrepid driver. Dave Turner, one of our managers, drove the second blue double-decker, and Malcolm Alden drove the red bus. We had decided to collect everyone from both the Chapter Road and the Cobbold Road factories in one round.

We were delighted to find that, with one or two exceptions, nearly all the workers were waiting to be picked up. Azadi Patel got on the first bus as usual, calm as always despite the fears of her husband. She said 'We are normal working-class people, and we just want to do our job. We don't want to bother anybody and we don't want anybody to bother us'.

Meena Ruperalia, a student from Willesden College, was also on the bus, with her sister. Meena is a sweet girl, made up like an Indian film star. She works at Grunwick during her college vacation every year, and has had to put up with a lot of ear-bashing from left-wing teachers, particularly those responsible for what is euphemistically called Liberal Studies. She came from Kenya eight years ago with her family, and her two brothers now run a sweet shop.

Carmelita, a nineteen-year-old girl from Jamaica, also caught the early bus. She says that her mother came in from doing night work about the time she got up and asked if she was going to work that day. Her father and mother had both tried to persuade her not to go, and in the course of the day her father phoned home several times to find out if there was word about her.

Jessie Patel, who came to Britain from Kenya in 1965, joined the first bus too. She, like the others, was used to the behaviour of the pickets by now. 'They behaved like wild animals,' she said. 'I wasn't frightened that day, but some people were very frightened and one girl actually fainted when we got to the factory—she is very nervous, but she still kept coming.'

The mood on the bus was tense, but everyone was determined to face out this day, which gave me a great feeling of pride, that I was associated with people who had so much courage. There was a feeling of comradeship, a feeling that we were all facing a common enemy.

The police advised us that we would not be able to get through to Chapter Road at this stage. So with a couple of police motor-cycles ahead of us and a police bus behind, we drove to Cobbold Road, where there were only sixty odd pickets. We got in there about 10 a.m. Before 12, we asked the police if we could get the Chapter Road workers to the other plant, and they thought this was a suitable time, since the pickets had gone off to assemble for a mass march against the company. So we drove through the back roads from Cobbold Road to Chapter Road. But we were spotted in the High Street by lookouts, and half way down Chapter Road we were confronted with a wall of pickets five or six men deep who looked like a seething mob of wild animals with a thin line of police trying to hold them back. The strain on the thin blue line of policemen was immense. I remember seeing a young policeman in the line with his helmet knocked off, straining with all his might to keep his arms linked with the policemen on each side of him. Other policemen ran from the factory gates and started pulling pickets away to relieve the pressure. Some pickets managed to get near the bus and stood in front of it to try to prevent it moving. A Police Sergeant pushed them aside and in so doing nearly unseated a police motor-cycle escort. The effect of police reinforcements enabled a wedge to be driven between the wall of pickets, and the picket lines eventually collapsed in two jumbled heaps on each side of the bus, enabling Ken to drive through to the safety of the factory. As we drove into the factory courtyard, there was a state of euphoria amongst the staff. One West

Indian woman named Loretta did a celebration dance in relief. While Arthur Scargill led his parade, we had shown that Grunwick was not going to be another Saltley. The rest of the day was relatively calm, and by the time the staff were ready to go home early that evening, there was no sign of the pickets.

On 11 July, seven of our van drivers appeared on the picket lines, carrying the banner of the TGWU. They claimed that they had secretly joined the union some time before, and had acted as spies against the management. I do not know what had persuaded them to come out; but I was particularly surprised that Kevin Slattery had joined the strike, since he had always been outspoken in his criticism of the unions. We subsequently dismissed these drivers—as we had dismissed the original strikers—for breach of contract. Advised by the union, they appealed to an industrial tribunal under Section 78 of the Employment Protection Act, claiming that they had been sacked for joining a union. On 6 August the industrial tribunal unanimously rejected their appeal.

11

Operation Pony Express

Even before the start of the mass picketing, the unions had begun to learn that Grunwick could not be stopped by lawful means. The efforts at a trade blockade, as well as the picketing of chemists that dealt with Grunwick, had failed to make a notable impact on our business. So a new attempt to black vital services to the company—electricity, water and gas as well as the post—was always on the cards. When the TUC gave its formal backing to the strike in March 1977, the blacking of these services was discussed. There was a little snag. We had already established that any attempt wilfully to interfere with the Royal Mail was a criminal offence, whether or not a Labour Attorney General would choose to prosecute it. Our lawyers advised us that any action taken to turn off electricity, gas or water would also be a criminal offence. But then, we were dealing with people for whom trade union power is more sacred than the law.

Tom Jackson had given an assurance in November that his union would take no further action to black our mails. Yet on the first day of the mass picketing, 13 June, he was quoted as saying 'If we can't crack Grunwick, we can't crack anything,' The following day, the Secretary for Industry, Eric Varley, declared his intention in Parliament of proposing amendments to the Post Office Act that would enable postal workers to interfere with the mail without incurring criminal prosecution.

On 16 June postal sorters at the Cricklewood branch office started blacking our mail. The local branch of the UPW is one of the most militant in the country. The day after the Cricklewood blacking began, Tom Jackson sent a telegram to the branch urging them to 'Work normally. Do not break the law.' This had no effect. That same day, Sam Silkin, the

Attorney General, rejected a formal appeal from the National Association for Freedom for him to intervene and end the blacking. This brought a ringing condemnation from the Conservative Shadow Attorney General, Sir Michael Havers, later that week: 'It means that the power of the unions is now so great in this particular case that where a clear breach of the law is happening, nothing can be done. That seems to me quite unacceptable.' Sir Keith Joseph and Lord Hailsham joined in the attack; it seemed that elements in the trade union movement, encouraged by the government, had reached the conclusion that they were able to break the law with impunity.

On 26 June the London District of the UPW, after meeting with Jack Dromey and Eddy Hayes, a member of the APEX executive, voted by 108 to 60 to step up the blacking of Grunwick mail and to take strike action if the Cricklewood postal sorters were disciplined by the Post Office. Dromey issued another of his pronunciamentos: 'This decision could halt the firm within forty-eight hours.' Roy Grantham welcomed this news as 'A step forward', but Tom Jackson—obviously embarrassed—said that the National Executive of the UPW would not make any actions of this kind official.

We had been placed in a very difficult situation. The government refused either to lift the statutory Post Office monopoly and enable private firms to deliver and collect the mail, or to take action to see that the Post Office carried out its duty to handle our mail—if necessary, by bringing in alternative staff. Meanwhile, undelivered packets of processed film were piling up inside the Chapter Road works. It was not until 29 June that Sir William Rylands, Post Office Chairman, said that the Cricklewood sorters would be sent home without pay if they refused to handle our mail as normal from 11.30 a.m. on 30 June. David Dodd, the UPW Branch Secretary at Cricklewood, insisted that he would not obey the law, backed up by the London District Council of the union, which threatened to call a strike if any of the Cricklewood sorters were disciplined. The contribution of the 'moderate' Tom Jackson, the union's General Secretary, was to dub the Post Office ultimatum as 'very foolish'. He announced that the UPW would pay the wages of the Cricklewood strikers if they were suspended. Under these circumstances, the Post Office threat evaporated into the offer of a paid holiday in the sun.

That same day, two left-wing MPs attempted to divert attention from the law breaking at Cricklewood by floating a red herring about the Grunwick accounts. Clinton Davis, the Under-Secretary for Trade, issued a written reply to questions from Ted Fletcher and John Lee, threatening Grunwick with prosecution if we remained in default in submitting our accounts for 1975 and 1976. This was a typical left-wing attempt at a diversionary smear. Our 1975 accounts had indeed been delayed, but had been posted through the Cricklewood sorting office where we were blacked, two weeks before. Our 1976 accounts had been posted the day before through the same sorting office only four months late—which is more than can be said for many trade unions. This could hardly be considered remiss for a company living in a state of siege, especially since delays of this kind are normal for private companies in a more routine situation.

There were renewed threats of the blacking of other vital services. Roy Grantham put out a statement saying that he had approached the electricians' union and the General and Municipal Workers' Union to cut off power and water to Grunwick. A new twist was a recommendation from the London Area Council of the National Union of Bank Employees (NUBE) that all finance to Grunwick should be blacked. It said that NUBE members at Willesdon should refuse to handle our accounts, and that other trade unions should withdraw their accounts if the bank continued to deal with Grunwick. Neither of these threats materialised.

But the continued postal blacking, against a company that does 84 per cent of its business by mail order, was a knife at the jugular. In the face of the intransigence of the Cricklewood sorters, the Post Office deferred its threatened suspension until Monday 4 July. Faced with renewed demands that the postmen who were breaking the law should be prosecuted, Silkin reiterated that he had no intention of taking any action against them. In the emergency debate in the House of Commons on 30 June, the Prime Minister appealed to the myth that the strikers had been dismissed from Grunwick for joining a trade union, and Albert Booth announced the setting up of a Court of Enquiry headed by Lord Justice Scarman—which was to prove to be merely another ploy to save the government's face and to divert attention from its failure to crack down on street violence and breaches of the criminal law. David Dodd, the Cricklewood organiser, seized on this to issue a statement that the blacking would only be stopped if the company would give an assurance that it would abide by the findings of the Court of Enquiry. What could be more reasonable than that? We were being asked, of course, to give a blank cheque to a panel that included the General Secretary of a union whose members were parading on the picket lines even as the Court of Inquiry began its researches, but which did not include a single representative of private business. I shall return to the Scarman report in a later chapter.

The Post Office's ultimatum to the Cricklewood sorters on Monday 4 July came and went. The deadline was set back yet again, to the following day, Tuesday. One encouraging piece of news on that Monday was that, under the influence of threatened legal action by NAFF and of appeals from Tom Jackson, the London District Council of the UPW announced that it would no longer support the blacking. Colin Maloney, the Branch Chairman of the Cricklewood UPW, expressed his bitter disappointment. But the withdrawal of support by London District did not stop the Cricklewood sorters voting to continue the blacking, by a majority of 63 against 41. On Tuesday the Post Office finally carried out its threat and suspended 26 sorters for refusing to handle Grunwick mail. The depot came to a total standstill. This produced limited sympathy strikes by union members at some other post offices in central London.

At first the Post Office action made little change in our lives. It mainly succeeded in exposing other businesses in the NW2 postal area to the same problems that we had suffered. The Cricklewood sorters made a great song and dance about how they were eager and willing to deliver other mail in the area, and made several attempts to do this, which resulted in the doors of the Cricklewood office being firmly locked. The simple fact of life for us was that, if a long time went by without our being able to get our mail out of the company, Grunwick would slowly be bled dry. Three weeks after the postal blacking began, there were nearly a thousand mail bags containing about a hundred thousand packets of processed mail piled up in every available corner in the Chapter Road works. There were also some bags at Cricklewood that we had been unable to retrieve. The contents of these bags represented about £250,000 in turnover. The Post Office action seemed to us to be largely theatrical. The Cricklewood sorters were not suffering, financially or otherwise. In effect, they had been given a paid vacation to continue spouting revolutionary slogans. We were suffering.

Once again, it was NAFF that came to the rescue. John Gouriet came to me that week and suggested that they should find people to take the mail and post it from letter boxes up and down the country. I was a little worried about the idea of all our mail going off into the wide blue yonder. I also wondered whether we should do at least part of the operation ourselves, even if it meant taking staff off production work. I was particularly concerned about the stamping of the envelopes, since I did not want anything to go out without the proper postage on it. But John's enthusiasm carried me along. I also felt, as he did, that there were many people around the country who were in sympathy with Grunwick and who would like to do something practical to help, and that it would be good to let some of them be involved. Here, after all, was a great opportunity for people to assist, in a perfectly peaceful and legal manner, to ensure that the trade union movement did not get away with illegal blacking. The more I considered this, the more enthusiastic I became.

On Thursday and Friday of that week a team of girls went out to buy stamps. The quantities involved were enormous, amounting in all to about £12,000. (Normally, of course, this mail would all have been dispatched without stamping through our postal licence.) A girl would breeze into a London post office, ask the clerk if they had 'plenty of stamps' and then slap in an order for £600 or £700 worth. Amazingly, the purchase of these huge quantities of stamps did not seem to raise anyone's suspicion. The operation began in total secrecy.

At 1 a.m. on Saturday 9 July I was waiting at Chapter Road for the arrival of a strange little convoy. As it rolled up to the gates, I could see a big forty-foot container lorry, two cars, a large box lorry and a minibus. All told, there were about twenty-five volunteers on board these oddly assorted vehicles, and they spent the next hour heaving our backlog of mail into the two lorries. The driver of the container lorry—who was himself a trade union member, a member of the TGWU—exclaimed that he had never seen his vehicle loaded so fast in the seven years that he had been on the road.

I watched the teams setting off again into the night at about 2.20 a.m. I am sure that what had been going on had not passed unobserved. Two of the volunteers say that they are sure they spotted lookouts as they drove down Chapter Road. We made little attempt to disguise the fact that something was going on at the factory: the lights were blazing, and police were in evidence in case of trouble. This makes it all the more surprising that we were able to maintain a total silence about the operation for the next three days.

The next phase of the operation—jocularly code-named 'Pony Express'—took place in a secret depot sixty miles from London. Over the weekend, more teams of supporters were assembled for what someone good-naturedly dubbed 'Operation Lick'. I can well imagine that stamping a hundred thousand envelopes by hand is not a joke, especially since every packet of our mail had to be individually weighed, and since the standard first class postage for many of our envelopes was 12½p, and the Post Office does not produce a 12½p stamp. The story was later put out that the volunteers, in their enthusiasm, had put the wrong postage on some of the envelopes. There is no evidence of this: every trial packet I saw was correctly stamped.

When the packets had been stamped, more volunteers moved in for the last phase of the operation. Drivers carried the mail, west, north and south, posting our envelopes in as many as ten thousand letterboxes as far north as Preston and Manchester and as far south as Plymouth and Truro.

So far, so good. We had beaten the ban at Cricklewood. The main worry now was that, when the news of Operation Pony Express leaked out, the Post Office Union might initiate a nationwide blacking of Grunwick mail. We had taken a calculated risk. We waited with bated breath to see how long it would take for the unions to hear about Pony Express. Although we could count on a certain proportion of the mail slipping through unnoticed, Grunwick was still using envelopes showing our brand name, so they were bound to be spotted before long.

The news began to break when some local sorting offices—first of all Luton, followed by Nottingham, and then a dozen or so others—noticed the brand names and started blacking the Grunwick mail. The first reporters to get onto the story were, unsurprisingly, from News Line, the daily paper of the Workers' Revolutionary Party, which has a number of friends at Cricklewood and seems to have useful contacts in other post offices as well.

When the details of Pony Express became public, there was a frenzied reaction from the left. There was much talk about a nationwide boycott of Grunwick mail; Dave Dodd, spokesman for the Cricklewood militants, declared that any post office that handled our mail 'would be dealing a direct blow to the Cricklewood black'. But by Tuesday morning we already had the evidence that plenty of post offices were letting the mail through. Fifty dummy envelopes, addressed to our own supporters, were sent off from post boxes up and down the country in order to gauge how much of the mail was getting through. By breakfast on Tuesday, more than a third of these had arrived. By Wednesday morning, thirty-four of them had got through. One postmaster actually rang up to say that his only complaint was that our mail was clogging up his letter boxes, and that he would be delighted, next time round, to take it in bulk. Against this backdrop, we were not overly worried that the UPW would again officially condone a breach of the criminal law. On the Tuesday Tom Jackson met with his executive. After nine hours of consultation, they could not make up their minds what to say.

The left-wing reaction to Pony Express was predictable, but still amusing. Mr Varley got up in the House of Commons on Tuesday afternoon to describe it as 'provocative'; he was howled down by Tory MPs. Many of the Tribunites sat with their mouths open in astonishment as John Gorst described the details of the operation and the quantity of mail that had been delivered for us.

The *Guardian* commented on its front page on Wednesday that the operation had been the most effective piece of 'strike-breaking, sanction-busting' since 1926. The same line was taken up in the Communist and Trotskyite papers. News Line exclaimed that Pony Express was 'one of the biggest peace time, strike-breaking provocations since 1926, the year of the General Strike'.

'It's the best thing since Entebbe', said one supporter on hearing the news. It was certainly a lifeline for Grunwick. The fort had been relieved in the nick of time. Ironically, it was now other businesses in the area which had nothing to do with our dispute that had to count the cost of the postmen's law-breaking. Harold Shaw, a Cricklewood businessman, issued a writ against the Post Office for failing to handle his mail. On 15 July Mr Justice MacKenna refused to make a High Court order requiring the Post Office to hand over mail held up in the Cricklewood Sorting Office. Mr Shaw appealed, but was again turned down. It appears that the High Court was unable to dispense justice due to immunities given to trade unions and to Public Corporations like the Post Office from Court actions by various Statutes.

The Cricklewood problem was not finally resolved until 24 July, when we were allowed to remove the bags of Grunwick mail that had been held up there for five weeks. This was described by the Post Office as an attempt to 'uncork the bottle'. We have not used Cricklewood since.

12

Albert Booth's fig leaf

The main role the government played in the Grunwick dispute was to attempt to deprive the company of its legal rights by duplicity rather than violence. The union and its supporters had come to understand that there is no law in the land that could compel us to reinstate the strikers against the wishes of our workforce. What the union had failed to achieve through rent-a-mob and the postal boycott, the government tried to achieve on its behalf through the Scarman report.

The government's partiality was always obvious. Three government ministers—Denis Howell, Shirley Williams and Fred Mulley—had turned up on the picket lines as early as May, to prove their support for trade union extremism. These were the 'moderates' described by Paul Johnson as 'broken butterflies', people who had forfeited any claim to represent a party that respected individual freedom by their subservience to the union that sponsored them and now demanded from them the same loyalty as a feudal seigneur might expect of a villein. The government was entirely committed to APEX. It had also shown that it would suspend the laws of England when they were broken by its union paymasters.

In the midst of the mass picketing in June, Albert Booth, the Secretary for Employment, was wheeled out to look for some way of reducing the government's embarrassment. He called on us to attend 'peace talks' with Roy Grantham and Jim Mortimer, the chairman of ACAS. We responded that, while we were always willing to talk to Mr Booth, the mob outside our factory gates made it difficult for us to move about town, and our position would be eased if the government would stop the riots. Merlyn Rees, the Home Secretary, conceded, the day after we gave this response, that 'it is a matter for concern that certain of those present [on the picket lines] may latch onto industrial action by a trade union as an excuse for breaches of the law, and particularly for violence against the police. This kind of activity has no place in responsible trade unionism.'

Encouraged by this, we sent off a letter to Silkin asking what steps he intended to take to prevent further breaches of the law. I also wrote to Albert Booth, observing that, in view of the evidence of cabinet bias and our legal appeal against the ACAS recommendation, which was still working its way through the courts, we saw little point in discussing the question of union recognition with the government. However, subject to our being physically able to get out of our factory, we were prepared to see him. I was particularly concerned that he should take the trouble to visit the plant and look at conditions for himself. He agreed to come to Grunwick, after meeting us.

So we went round to St James's Square to see Albert Booth for the first time on 23 June. Mr Booth is not much of a law-and-order man. Our first suggestion was that he should take some action to stop the violence and restore our mail. It seemed that he was not keen to do anything unless we signed on the dotted line and gave APEX what it wanted. He did not seem interested in what our workers felt. Instead, he pushed the idea of a court of inquiry.

He was unable to explain to us how such a body would relieve the illegal pressures that were being brought to bear on the company—or how it could fail to conflict with the courts that would be considering our appeal against ACAS. I urged him to come to Grunwick and see what the situation was like for himself. He appeared distinctly unenthusiastic. This hardly raised our confidence, since we had been given to understand that Booth would visit Grunwick after our meeting and it seemed that this had just been a ploy to get us into his office. After Grantham's reception by the staff, however, I can see that Booth must have been nervous about testing the feelings of a workforce whose livelihoods had been threatened—and whose daily lives had been disrupted—by the union laws he was backing.

We thought hard and long about the suggested court of inquiry. One argument that we had to consider was that if Grunwick agreed to cooperate with a court of inquiry set up by the government for political purposes, we might be regarded as conferring some kind of legitimacy on it. On the other hand, if we refused to cooperate, it would be said that we were afraid of having the causes and circumstances of the dispute investigated. Our critics would use this in their efforts to make out that the extravagant calumnies put about by APEX and the strikers were true.

We knew how little chance there was that Mr Booth's court of inquiry would produce a report that ran counter to APEX interests. In proposing his court, Mr Booth was seeking a fig leaf to cover the government's naked support for trade union bullying—which had become politically embarrassing since it was obviously losing Labour votes. With a learned judge as its chairman, such a panel could be expected to impress public opinion as impartial, even magisterial. Yet its findings would have no force in law, and it would not be required to conduct its affairs according to the normal strict procedural rules of a real court. Was there any reason to doubt that the whole thing would amount to an elaborate charade, intended to mask the government's hope of imposing the union's terms on Grunwick?

Still, we knew that we could only gain by cooperating in a thorough investigation of the causes of the dispute. We had nothing to hide. We knew that the factual evidence about life at Grunwick would put paid to the poisonous lies assiduously circulated by our enemies. We could only win on the evidence; we could only lose from the findings of a political inquiry set up by a partisan minister. So we resolved to cooperate with any court of inquiry that Mr Booth might set up, but we refused to be bound by any recommendations it might see fit to make. We also stressed that we would only be able to cooperate with the court of inquiry so far as our attendance at the High Court and the picketing situation outside the company would permit, and that we were not prepared under any circumstances to reinstate the strikers who had been lawfully dismissed.

We went back to St James's Square on 27 June for a second, seemingly interminable session with Albert Booth. This time he wanted us to give a blank cheque to a mediator he proposed to appoint. We struggled to explain to him that the stand we had taken was based on principle, the expressed wishes of our workers, and the laws of England, and that we did not see why we should disregard all of these and place our company in the hands of someone who, at the best, would be assigned to split the difference between right and wrong.

We did not seem to be getting very far with Mr Booth, so I said that I would like to put an example to him. 'Let us suppose,' I said, 'that you have a very pretty wife and I come up and say that I have fallen in love with her and that she's a very desirable woman. I want to share your wife with you—say Tuesdays, Thursdays and Saturdays—and you can have her for the rest of the week. I am sure you would tell me that you were not very impressed by this suggestion. So I would say to you that we have an honest disagreement of opinion concerning your wife and that we should refer the matter to a mediator. Of course, if you are any sort of husband, you will refuse point blank to have a mediator, because this type of disagreement is not susceptible to mediation. It's the same with Grunwick.' Mr Booth looked shocked.

Three days later, Booth named the members of his court of inquiry. It was to consist of Lord Justice Scarman, Pat Lowry, the personnel manager of British Leyland, and Terence Parry, the general secretary of the Fire Brigade Union. It was striking that there was no representative of private business on this panel—still less of the 800,000 small businessmen in the country who were best-equipped to understand the problems of a company like ours and who contribute so much to production and employment. Parry, a left-winger, was an odd choice in view of the fact that members of his union were in the picket lines outside our factory gates; this gave rise to some brusque exchanges between him and me in the course of the hearings. The record of industrial relations at British Leyland is less than impressive, and I doubt whether Mr Lowry—although an honourable man—is any better qualified to offer advice on the affairs of my company than I am on his.

The partisan composition of the court was pointed out in a vigorous editorial in the *Daily Telegraph*. Readers of the *Sun* were unable to study its reaction that day, since members of the National Graphical Association blacked it because they objected to the headline 'Now call off the mob'.

We stuck to the original decision; we would happily give evidence to the Scarman panel, but we would not be bound to accept its findings. it held a preliminary session in the Piccadilly Hotel on 5 July, and decided that the hearings would start on 11 July and that the Brent Trades Council, in addition to APEX and the company, would be represented. It was not an auspicious date, since that was the day that had been chosen for mass action designed to bring the company to a halt. I had heard that Scargill and others were talking about bringing up to 25,000 pickets to London. We appealed to the Scarman court to postpone its hearing so that we would be able to attend from the first day. Our request was turned down, so the hearings began without us.

The Scarman hearings extended over ten days. On 5 July Lord Scarman explained that 'we can make recommendations but we cannot make any orders. This is an exercise in informing public opinion.' The rules of court would not apply: there would be no oaths, no possibility of perjury charges against people who told lies (and therefore no guarantee that everyone would tell the truth).

Plenty of the myths were rehearsed during the first few days, when Counsel for APEX, presented the union's case, followed by Counsel for the Brent Trades Council. Roy Grantham made a long statement about the 'moderation' of his union and the reactionary union-bashing temperament of the company it was trying to coerce. He made some remarkable statements about me, describing me as 'a most

unusual ... very reactionary employer. ... In my experience
as a senior trade union official and indeed through my
working life as a trade unionist, I have never come across a
company which has been so averse to the normal procedures
of conciliation and negotiation as Grunwick'.

Some interesting points emerged from APEX's testimony.
Indira Misty, one of the girls who joined the walk-out,
dropped a hint that she knew the strike was going to start two
weeks before it actually did. This fed our suspicion that the
whole thing may have been a put-up job. She was particularly
confused about the low wage rates that we had supposedly
paid. She talked about her miserable pay, but then conceded
under cross-examination that, with overtime, she was
probably taking home £64 a week.

Another APEX witness, Delcie Claire, who walked out of
the firm on 10 June, the Friday before mass picketing began,
admitted that she was getting £9 more on the picket lines
than she had been earning for part-time work with Grunwick
before. So much for what Jack Dromey described as 'the
romantic passion' that brought people out to join the pickets.

The language of the APEX people echoed their enduring
amazement that they had come up against an employer who
would not accept the divine right of union officials. Len
Gristey, Grantham's senior London organiser, told the court
that he did not believe that we enjoyed the right not to talk to
APEX if we did not choose to do so.

On the fifth day of the hearings Tom Durkin and Jack
Dromey appeared. Durkin made little effort to keep his
left-wing leanings a secret. 'In all frankness,' he said, 'we
should make it clear that there are many voices raised in the
community and trade union movement which say that rather
than allow Grunwick and the National Association for
Freedom to thwart the exercise of a fundamental trade union
right ... these workplaces should be taken over and run as
cooperative enterprises.' Lord Scarman fielded this one
neatly. 'It is very unlikely,' he observed, 'that an institution
such as a cooperative enterprise would have found the energy,
imagination and the capital to start and develop Grunwick.

They might have the will to take it over once somebody has started it.'

When Durkin was asked whether he would insist on union recognition if a majority was opposed to it, he replied 'We would still try to get a trade union presence. ... The union concerned might take a different view but we would still seek to get a trade union presence.'

Jack Dromey plunged into a long political tirade that provoked Lord Scarman into interjecting "Most of this is pure politics and has nothing whatever to do with this inquiry.' When Lord Scarman put it to him that it would be understandable, in view of the way he behaved, if some people described him as 'an agitator,' he agreed that this was so.

The remark that particularly dwells in my mind from what was said on that fifth day was used by both Durkin and Dromey. They both compared the people who walked out in August 1976 to 'chickens out of a coop'. It is not a very polite analogy.

At long last we got our chance to present Grunwick's version of the case. We were disappointed that a number of our workers were denied access to the Court of Inquiry on the grounds that their evidence was considered unnecessary and would only delay the completion of the Inquiry. We were also perplexed that the evidence from the director of the Photographic Careers Centre—which has been summarised in an earlier chapter—was not admitted either, since this was testimony from an impeccably independent source that Grunwick wage rates were either comparable to or better than those in other photo-finishing firms that can be properly compared to us. Still, we were able to put the record straight on many contentious points, and this came through in the report that the Scarman Court of Inquiry finally produced.

As we expected, the recommendations of the report were in the main at complete odds with its findings on the facts. The report was unable even to give a coherent account of what had started the dispute. According to the Scarman document, it remained 'difficult to define with precision what the

grievances were'. The image of Grunwick as a sweatshop, run
by a nineteenth-century employer was shattered for good by
the details of wages and conditions that the Scarman panel
had had to consider. But this did not prevent the Scarman
court from recommending the reinstatement of the strikers,
and suggesting union recognition at some time in the
future—a question which Scarman specifically declared to lie
outside his court's terms of reference.

We were further irked by the fact that the Scarman report
was leaked prior to publication. It was published on Thursday
23 August. In that morning's *Guardian* and *Times* there were
accurate summaries of the report, which was supposedly
embargoed until 2.30 p.m. that day. Still more disturbing was
the evidence that trade union officials intimately involved in
the dispute had had access to the report even earlier.
Remarks by Tudor Thomas, Grantham's number two, that
were quoted in the *News of the World* on the previous
Sunday suggested that he had either seen an advance copy of
the report or was endowed with considerable prophetic gifts.
We had to wait to receive our copy until after the *Guardian*
and *The Times* had already told the world what it contained.

For this reason, we were not anxious to be rushed into
issuing an immediate statement. APEX and the strikers were
both jubilant and threatening. Roy Grantham said 'If Ward
doesn't accept, then we will look to other methods'. Jack
Dromey announced 'The report is a basis for a solution. If
Grunwick accepts, it has a future. If it does not, it has none'.

We went round to St James's Square at 4.45 that
afternoon for yet another session with Albert Booth. He
began by apologising for the leaks and said that he would
conduct an inquiry. Our line was that we had come to listen
to Booth rather than to have a discussion, since we had not
been favoured by a leak and so had not had time to study the
report, let alone consult with the workforce.

Booth hammered on about reinstatement. We tripped him
up several times by pinpointing the contradictions in the
Scarman report. For example, Scarman suggested the
possibility that the company might re-employ some of the

strikers and make ex-gratia payments to others. But might this not land Grunwick with the problem of a striker who could reject both alternatives and go hunting for hefty compensation via the industrial courts? Again, if the reinstatement of the strikers was to be staggered over several months—maybe right into the summer of 1978, when new vacancies would start opening up again—might not those left to languish become very frustrated?

Patently, Mr Booth had not thought deeply on these matters. Anyway, he said, all these details could be left to a mediator. As before, he gave us no clue to who this mediator might be, and therefore no guarantee of his impartiality.

We asked him to tell us what he thought would happen if the company rejected the Scarman report. Booth said he foresaw a new escalation of the conflict, and a return to mass picketing, unlawful acts, and so on. This was born out by the statement of the Strike Committee. If the company was so 'intransigent' as to refuse to forfeit its legal rights, then the unions would be 'compelled' to put on the frighteners. Under these circumstances, of course, the unions 'could not be held responsible' for anything that might happen.

In the room with Albert Booth we gingerly put forward our alternative scenario. Was it impossible to persuade APEX and the TUC to drop the attitude that their manhood was in doubt if they failed to win *every* dispute? Couldn't Mr Grantham bring himself to say 'Ah well, we've lost this one, we can't win them all. Time to go home.' This was also wasted on Mr Booth.

With the bank holiday looming up, we agreed that the company would take a week or so to consider its reply, and that we might meet again the following week. As we left, we noticed that Roy Grantham was still hanging about outside. He had been to see Mr Booth earlier on, and had lingered, obviously waiting for some signal as to what our response had been.

I went off for a quiet weekend to think things over. After the break, I met with the workers at both Chapter Road and Cobbold Road to discuss the Scarman proposals with them.

They left me in no doubt that they were annoyed that I had even thought it necessary to discuss the report with them: they felt that it should have been rejected out of hand, and that their opinion—which they had demonstrated in two independent opinion polls already—should be taken as a foregone conclusion. I spent most of my time reassuring them that they need have no fear that I would weaken under political pressure. An Irish girl named Mary Fitzgerald who approached me in the mail order department reflected the prevailing mood. 'Mr Ward,' she said, 'I understand that this Scarman report is suggesting a mediator. My suggestion is, please would you just let that mediator come into the works and we'll take care of him.' The staff were all angry that Scarman had played down their opinions, as if the only workers who count are union members.

I met with the other directors the same day. To a man, they wanted to turn down the main proposals in the Scarman report. We agreed that instead of issuing a short press release we should produce a considered and detailed account of our reasons for rejection. We also agreed that if there were any points in the Scarman report that we could possibly accept without running counter to the wishes of the workforce, we would do so.

On Thursday, we made the 'Counter-Scarman' report public. It was reprinted in full in *The Times* and the *Telegraph*, accompanied by very sympathetic editorials. I think it is worth reprinting in full, because it sums up the whole Grunwick position, as well as the corporatist philosophy that has led not only Scarman but the whole country, astray.

THE 'COUNTER-SCARMAN' REPORT

When the Secretary of State for Employment, using the powers conferred upon him by Section 4 of the Industrial Courts Act 1919, established an Inquiry headed by The Rt. Hon. Lord Justice Scarman OBE, with Mr J. P. Lowry and

Mr T. Parry CBE, OBE, as the other members, he directed that the terms of reference to the Court should be as follows:

'To inquire into the causes and circumstances of, and relevant to, the dispute, other than any matter before the High Court, until the final determination of those proceedings, and to report.'

This was in itself a very peculiar remit, because few concerned citizens could have been unaware that Grunwick was in dispute with former employees whom it had dismissed and who were represented by APEX. Fewer still could have failed to notice the course the dispute had taken. To follow its instructions, all the Court of Inquiry needed to do was to reproduce newspaper coverage of the dispute, which would have informed the Secretary of State of all that had happened and the differing standpoints of the protagonists.

Of course nobody supposed that the Court of Inquiry had so restricted a function. It had been established for a political purpose. It had no legal authority, took no evidence from witnesses on oath, and because it was in haste to produce a report, limited the number of witnesses it heard. Its job was to resolve a dispute which was embarrassing the Government. A Court of Inquiry is decked out in the majestic trappings of the law, without having any legal authority and without having to obey the normal requirements of a court.

Grunwick was therefore, from the outset, presented with a difficult choice. The Government was not an impartial observer of the dispute. It had given complete backing to APEX. In all discussions with Grunwick management the Government had urged it to capitulate to the strikers. Three Government ministers had joined the APEX picket line outside Grunwick. It was beyond belief that a Government committed so completely to APEX had established an Inquiry that it thought would produce a report hostile to that trade union's interests.

On the other hand, if Grunwick refused to cooperate with the Court of Inquiry, the wider political purposes for which the Inquiry had been set up would at once be discounted. It would be claimed that the only function of the Inquiry was to determine the causes and circumstances of the dispute. By refusing cooperation, Grunwick would be held to be afraid to have such causes and circumstances investigated. That in turn would be transformed into an admission that the extravagant calumnies put abroad by APEX and the strikers were true.

Another consideration affected Grunwick's decision to cooperate. The Company had little doubt that any Inquiry would reject the APEX version of how the strike started. Even if the recommendations bore little relation to the evidence, the demolition of a carefully constructed edifice of falsehood, which had gained widespread currency because of constant repetition, must have an impact on public opinion.

Grunwick therefore offered the Court of Inquiry its complete cooperation in determining the causes and circumstances of the dispute and fulfilling its instructions from the Secretary of State. But Grunwick refused to be bound by any recommendations the Inquiry might make that went beyond its terms of reference.

Grunwick believes the wisdom of the course of action it took will be apparent to those who read the report of the Court of Inquiry. The evidence, as expected, favours Grunwick. The recommendations, as expected, do not.

The philosophy of the report of the Court of Inquiry

Before commenting in detail on the Report, Grunwick thinks it will be helpful to explain its attitude towards the philosophy that lies behind the Report.

It is not a philosophy based upon malice, nor upon a desire to sanctify an injustice. Put baldly, it is the philosophy of the Corporate State. The Report does not of course claim that English law has yet benefited from the legislation needed to sustain a corporate state and that Grunwick are lawbreakers for defying such enactments. On the contrary, the Report makes constant references to Grunwick's scrupulous observance of the law and praises the Company for this. But the praise is qualified by an occasional reference to the 'letter of the law', and there are several references to the 'spirit of the law', or even more vaguely to the 'policy of the law'. Grunwick is held to have behaved according to the 'letter of the law' but somehow to have fallen short of apprehending the niceties of 'the policy of the law', as the Government and powerful vested interests would wish that policy to be.

But when this 'policy of the law' is examined, it turns out to have nothing to do with law of any description and everything to do with conciliating the trade unions. It is the trade unions themselves who have most strenuously insisted that as little law as possible be applied to trade disputes. They have been unwilling to allow the law in these matters to become coherent, or to apply to a whole range of cases that are of daily occurrence in British Industry. Their assumption has been that the law would compel them to honour bargains and regulate their activities in a way they find uncongenial, or adverse to their interests. Thus it is a very strange argument that arrives at the conclusion that where the law is not on the side of trade unions, businessmen owe it to the community to interpret it as if it were.

Such an assumption is in every way appropriate to a corporate state, where individuals consent to, or are compelled to consent to, having their interests represented by associations. In such a state, Government, employers' associations, and trade unions decide what industrial policy should be. Individuals are not allowed to disturb the symmetry of these arrangements by any inconvenient appeal to natural rights. The group decides for the individual. If any additional legal force is required to coerce the recalcitrant, a new enactment, often with retrospective provisions, is passed in short order.

Though Britain has been moving towards these tripartite arrangements, they have not yet been given the force of law, or indeed of popular approval. Unfortunately the Report of the Court of Inquiry tends to underplay this fact. It takes no account of the wishes of the existing Grunwick workforce, because it equates workers best interests with trade union representation. It believes that Grunwick has sometimes acted 'unreasonably', because a refusal to accommodate the

desires of a Government and trade unions, especially when no
approval for such a refusal is sought from any trade
association, obviously struck the three members of the Court
of Inquiry as perverse.

Grunwick wishes to make it clear that it claims the right to
dissent from corporatist political assumptions. Perhaps
Britain would be happier if the individual has less freedom,
though Grunwick does not think so. But it is a matter for the
British people as a whole through their representatives in
Parliament and not for Courts of Inquiry. So long as an area
of freedom still exists, a good citizen has every right to enjoy
it: he ought not to be dissuaded by being told that the
exercise of his undoubted rights is irritating powerful groups,
who desire him to act in a manner better suited to the
advancement of their interests.

The start of the dispute

Grunwick has little to contest in the Report's explanation of
how the dispute began, except that the Court of Inquiry
nowhere gives sufficient weight to the evidence it accepts.

The dispute began when Mr Devshi Bhudia, aged 19,
walked off the job. From the start, Grunwick maintained that
this was a premeditated action by someone who had nothing
to lose and whose only concern was to cause an industrial
dispute. This has repeatedly been denied and various fanciful
accounts of what occurred have gained currency. But the
Report puts the matter quite clearly on page 6.

'There was an element of predetermination in Mr Bhudia's
departure. He had become discontented with pay and
conditions and a week earlier had discussed with some the
possibility of joining a union. He had carried his dissatis-
faction sufficiently far to seek and obtain the promise of a job
elsewhere before, *on his own admission,* he provoked the
incident which brought his dismissal.'

That should establish beyond doubt that Mr Bhudia
wanted to be dismissed and the question that arises is why?
Again the Report very clearly explains the facts—facts which

Grunwick has been asserting and the strikers denying since the beginning of the dispute.

Mrs Jayaben Desai, who subsequently became the strike leader, was not dismissed at all. As the report says on page 7. 'There was an altercation and Mrs Desai asked for her cards and walked out.'

But Mrs Desai, who had asked for her cards, and Mr Bhudia, who found another job and then contrived his own dismissal, did not leave the matter there. On the following Monday morning they were outside Grunwick with placards. The Report explains what happened.

'At the lunch hour Mr Sunil Desai and very probably some others arranged with sympathisers, most of them working in the mail order department, for an afternoon walk-out. It was timed for 3.00 pm; about 50 walked out. When the party from inside reached the street, there was shouting and excitement, and an inconclusive parley with management. The strikers decided to march round to Cobbold Road. When they arrived there, a violent scene ensued. The strikers were calling upon those who were inside to come out and join them. *Some fiery spirits tried to force an entry and broke some windows.'*

So far, so good, and we might reasonably expect on the basis of this evidence that the Report would state that the dispute was contrived and that Grunwick very properly dismissed those who were intent upon destroying its property.

But the Report draws no such conclusion from the evidence. It does not think Grunwick should have paid much attention to the incident, on the incredible grounds that, 'Although there was some violence, it was short-lived.'

If industrial relations are to be conducted on this basis, then the ordinary rule of law has no place in them. Football supporters, who after the excitement of a match kicked in some shop windows, would not escape punishment in court by pleading, 'Although there was some violence, it was short-lived.'

Here we are not dealing with legal punishment, but only with the universally admitted right of an employer to dismiss an employee for misconduct. Yet according to the Report, an employer should not dismiss for misconduct an employee who commits an act that would be punishable in a court of law.

These are strange standards indeed, and Grunwick rejects them out of hand. We believe the Report, at this point, is seriously in error, illogical in its reasoning, dangerous in its implications, and arguing contrary to custom and practice—not to mention commonsense.

Grunwick and Trade Unions

The attitude of Grunwick to trade unions has been the source of deliberate misrepresentation from the time the dispute began. It is not exaggerating the matter to say, that many within the trade union movement would have taken little account of the dispute, were it not for the constant repetition of the single most important claim of the strikers—that they were dismissed for joining a trade union.

So the findings of the Court of Inquiry on this point, set out on pages 9–10, are of paramount importance. Though Grunwick believes that the findings do less than justice to the management's attitude, they dispose so effectively of the false claim that workers were dismissed for joining a trade union that the passage is worth quoting.

'Since the company's attitude to unions has been the subject of discussion before us, it is right that we should state our finding explicitly. It was the desire of the directors and top management of the company, while professing to accept the right of individual employees to join a trade union, not to recognise a union for collective bargaining purposes; and they have sought up to this day to maintain that policy. They successfully resisted an attempt by the Transport and General Workers Union to secure recognition in 1973, when a few workers (some 16, we are told) came out on strike in support of two who had been made redundant. They have sought up to this day to maintain their non-union shop. To this end they have established a works committee, and taken steps to ensure good physical working conditions. Management is 'from the front', in the sense that managers are always accessible and visible. Money has been spent on maintaining the premises in excellent condition—Chapter Road, in particular, into which the company moved in April 1976, after extensive modernisation. We do, however, accept Mr Ward's statement that, if the company's workforce, or a substantial proportion of it, should evince a wish to be represented by a union, the company would not resist recognition. We also accept his word that the company recognises the right of every employee to join a union, if he chooses. Nevertheless the company, we are sure, does all that it can to persuade its employees that they are better placed without a union. There is, we stress, nothing unlawful in the company's attitude towards unionisation: but whether in all the circumstances it remains today reasonable is another question—perhaps the fundamental question confronting us.'

Grunwick does less to persuade its workers against joining trade unions than the report allows. Nevertheless the vital point, that the company would not resist recognition if the workforce desired it and accepts the right of individual workers to join trade unions, was accepted by the Court of Inquiry.

Where Grunwick might take issue with the Report, if it more clearly understood what was meant, occurs in the phrase, 'but whether in all the circumstances it remains today reasonable is another question—perhaps the fundamental question confronting us'.

In what sense is it less 'reasonable', not to wish to join an association, than to wish to do so? If the law permits an employee not to join a union, why is he unreasonable in exercising that right? And what are the 'circumstances' that 'today' make it unreasonable, or perhaps injudicious, for employees not to join unions and for management to refuse to persuade them to do so?

The passage is too opaque to give any indication of precisely what is meant. Grunwick feels that the underlying implication is that in 1977, trade union power is so great, that one is most unwise to resist it too strenuously, or to expect it to observe the circuimspection and restraints that are

required from everyone else. If that is the meaning, then it is
the authentic voice of the Corporate State. Grunwick
unhesitatingly rejects it. Trade unions already enjoy vast
legal immunities and in pursuing industrial aims can do more
or less as they please. If on top of this, companies are to be
deemed unreasonable for exercising what authority they have
left and using what little legal protection remains to them,
then no society can exist in Britain, other than a collectivist
one.

The Court of Inquiry and the Grunwick workforce

Nobody has ever denied that the overwhelming majority of
Grunwick workers do not wish to be represented by APEX,
or to have the strikers reinstated. The Court of Inquiry did
not set a precedent by disputing this fact.

Obviously the MORI and Gallup ballots impressed the
Inquiry. It referred to MORI, on page 13 as 'an independent
body of undoubted integrity'. About the Gallup ballot it was
even more explicit, on page 15.

'But there is no evidence that Mr Ward exerted pressure
on his workforce in respect of this poll: and we are satisfied
that he was content to allow the situation as it was in July to
exert its own pressures upon the company's employees.'

Though perhaps expressed in a somewhat cumbersome,
and even grudging way, this is the clearest possible
recognition that the democratic decision of the Grunwick
workforce is set firmly against the strikers and their demands.

Whereupon the Grunwick workers' decision disappears
from the pages of the Report and is never again mentioned,
either directly, or by implication!

Grunwick find this perhaps the most astonishing aspect of
the Report. Page after page is devoted to the opinions,
thoughts and wishes of APEX. Numerous aspects of the
dispute are probed, but no reference is made to the Grunwick
workforce, nor any comment offered as to how the
management is supposed to reconcile them to the presence of
a trade union they do not want, and the reinstatement of
those who have, to put it mildly, been making their lives

unpleasant and their jobs insecure. It is as if, for the Inquiry, the Grunwick workers did not exist.

Grunwick does not believe that this omission is accidental. The workers' opinions are inconvenient, because they do not support the APEX demands. We do not mean that the Inquiry took a conscious decision to ignore them. The fault lies in the whole corporatist attitude of the Inquiry. Workers who do not want to be represented by trade unions must be strange fish indeed. The Inquiry was so convinced that the role of trade unions in industry is wholly beneficent, so concerned to have APEX strikers back inside Grunwick, that instinctively it shied away from examining the most important piece of evidence in front of it, because the plain meaning of the evidence was to contradict flatly its own intellectual preconceptions.

We believe the Inquiry erred badly on this point. By failing to examine the intensity of the Grunwick workforce's rejection of the strikers' claims it makes nonsense of its principal recommendation. The existing workforce simply would not tolerate the re-employment of the strikers. Not to understand that, is not to understand why the dispute has gone on for so long.

Working conditions at Grunwick

There is no doubt that the Report has performed a most valuable public service by disposing of the slanders and libels about working conditions at Grunwick, which were the substance of the APEX case.

The Inquiry, on page 10, quotes from the General Secretary of APEX, Mr Roy Grantham's speech to the 1976 TUC Conference.

'A reactionary employer taking advantage of race and employing workers on disgraceful terms and conditions.'

No more vile charge could be imagined, and in making it Mr Grantham was employing another trade union immunity, the one that frees unions from the legal consequences of acts, when such acts are in furtherance of a trade dispute.

Mr Grantham, as he so frequently explains, is a moderate.

Far worse has been alleged by the Grunwick Strike Committee, the Brent Trades Council, the Socialist Workers Party and other participants on the picket line, who are not moderates and who would be insulted if they were so called.

But when the Report is read, what remains of the talk about 'a nineteenth-century sweatshop', 'abominable working conditions', 'workers treated like animals', to quote but a few of the steady stream of lies put out on behalf of the strikers?

The Inquiry says, on page 19:

'When one turns to working conditions, the same sort of picture emerges. Physical working conditions were reasonably good, and at Chapter Road, save for the mischance with the air conditioning in a hot summer, excellent.'

'Reasonably good', all the way up to, 'excellent'. Hardly the picture painted by APEX and the strikers.

But what of the intolerable oppression of working compulsory overtime in the busy summer months, which the company writes into contracts of employment and which is offset by the very easy pace worked, even during normal hours, throughout the rest of the year?

The Inquiry says, on page 19:

'Compulsory overtime was at times a burden, but more often seen as a welcome addition to the wage packet.'

But what about those strikers who were humiliated daily, by having to hold up their hands to go to the lavatory? That never happened either. What did happen is explained by the Inquiry, on page 17.

'Asking for permission to go to the lavatory, a requirement which had been imposed at Station Road, Wembley, when the lavatories were *outside the premises occupied by the company*, but was never imposed after the move to Chapter Road.'

Like all other well-run companies, Grunwick wanted to know if any employees left the premises during working hours, but, of course, it has never expected its workers to seek permission to visit lavatories.

That leaves intact very little of the strikers' case. As indeed the Inquiry concedes, though it has an explanation. It says, on page 15, speaking of the strikers' attitudes.

'While it remains difficult to define with precision what the grievances were, the evidence leaves us in no doubt of the fact that they were felt. Of course, it does not follow that because they were felt they were justified.'

Quite so. Grunwick would like to ask: Whoever heard of a dispute of this length, pursued with this degree of violence, accompanied by so much anti-management propaganda of which it could be said, 'it remains difficult to define with precision what the grievances were'?

The Inquiry and the Brent Trades Council

An answer to the question posed in the last paragraph might have been forthcoming, if the Inquiry had looked more closely at the composition, and role in the dispute, played by the Brent Trades Council.

The Inquiry agrees that Mr Jack Dromey, the Secretary of the Brent Trades Council, 'provided substantial support for the strike and exercised great influence upon the strikers, all of whom were ill-acquainted with the conduct of industrial relations in Britain ... ' (page 8). The point unfortunately is pursued no further.

Grunwick wishes to predict that much more will be heard of Mr Jack Dromey, whose views as expressed to the Court of Inquiry on the issues of our day and age will become increasingly apparent. It will be of particular interest to see how Mr Dromey's relations with APEX and the TUC develop.

Grunwick and grievances

Where Grunwick is disposed to accept a measure of criticism contained in the Report is in respect of its grievance procedure.

The Inquiry says, on page 15 of its Report:

'If there be no adequate ways and means of handling grievances, even fanciful ones can pose serious industrial problems.'

The Inquiry is stating a general proposition and not accusing Grunwick of having no means of dealing with grievances. Nevertheless, it is critical of the procedures that existed at the time the dispute began.

Grunwick will not plead all the difficulties that it has encountered in this sphere. It accepts that there was room for improvement in its grievance procedure. Everything has been done to make certain that no similar complaint can be made in the future.

Grunwick does not for a moment believe that any employee was unjustly treated, but has changed its procedure so that even the suspicion that this might be so has been obviated. We accept that in industrial relations the 'fanciful' element can play a part.

Grunwick wishes to have a bargaining relationship with its workers that accepts them as industrial partners in a productive enterprise. Perhaps, the courage and loyalty of the Grunwick workforce will be accepted as evidence that this relationship is well understood on the shop-floor.

Grunwick and the Court of Inquiry's recommendations

As will be apparent from the foregoing, Grunwick does not believe that the recommendations of the Inquiry follow from the evidence that the Inquiry accepted.

It might have been better if the Inquiry had pursued its original intention and made no reference to admitted trade union illegalities. The censure of the Inquiry upon trade unions for law-breaking is couched in such terms as to make probable a repetition of the offence, and gives no hope to those who would wish to see official bodies at least attempt to differentiate between those who break the law and those who are at pains to observe it.

Where possible Grunwick will meet the recommendations of the Inquiry; but regrettably the eccentric nature of the Report, its heavily corporatist prejudices, its equation of opposites, and its inability to pronounce authoritatively on matters of principle that cannot be pushed aside in the interests of peace at any price, make the extent to which Grunwick can bind itself, severely limited.

Grunwick will accept the second of the three recommendations set forth on page 23 of the Report. As the company explained to the Inquiry it has always been prepared to allow any employee who wishes it, to have a trade union bargain on his or her behalf. We have no hesitation in re-affirming this declaration and thus complying with recommendation (2).

Recommendation (3) is not a recommendation at all, but merely a comment upon the role of trade unions as seen by the Inquiry. We have made our views clear on this matter. Grunwick will recognise APEX as having the right to bargain for such members of the existing workforce as wish to join it, if the House of Lords overturns the judgement of the Court of Appeal.

Recommendation (1) Grunwick rejects in its entirety. Never under any circumstances will the company reinstate those who were, very properly, dismissed. The suggestion is completely impracticable, as the existing Grunwick workforce would never accept it. Additionally, Grunwick believes that reinstatement would be a surrender to rampant illegality, brute force, and the coercive power of a mighty vested interest that seeks not to reason, but to compel.

The suggestion that ex-gratia payments be made to strikers upon recommendation of a mediator, confirms Grunwick's impression, derived from earlier sections of the Report, that the Court of Inquiry does not understand the provisions of the Employment Protection Act, nor is it fully cognisant of the way industrial tribunals determine cases. Grunwick rejects any such suggestion of payments to those who by their own actions terminated their employment.

The issue of determining supposed vacancies therefore does not arise. Grunwick has acted within the law, both in letter and spirit. It will not abandon its legal rights and is shocked that it should be asked to do so.

If, by illegal action, the company is forced out of business, it will accept its fate, in the hope that such a fate will arouse public opinion to demand better protection from the authorities for those who legally go about their business. Grunwick, if it is ruined by illegal coercion will generously recompense its loyal workforce and go into liquidation. But the company believes it will survive and prosper. If it does not, it will bear that, rather than submit and give another hostage to an iniquitous tyranny.

On the same day that we issued the 'Counter-Scarman Report', I published an article in *The Times* that gave a more personal account of my view of the Scarman report.

That same evening Sir Keith Joseph levelled a devastating attack on the report before a packed audience in Hove. He declared, 'the unions are not automatically the oppressed. It is sometimes the employer, the job-creator, who is oppressed. Indeed, it is sometimes the non-union members who are oppressed—by the unions.' Sir Keith drew the contrast between the Scarman who had lent his name to this report and the Scarman who delivered the splendid lectures upholding the role of judges as defenders of universal law—as opposed to partisan legislation—that were published under the title *English Law—The New Dimension* in 1975.

After we gave our response to the Scarman report Albert Booth said that the company 'has a great deal to answer for.' His friends at the TUC took up the theme at their annual conference in Blackpool. They were a bit delayed in getting round to the emergency motion on Grunwick, however, because of the circus games that were played out by a little pub managers' union and the mighty TGWU who were locked in a territorial dispute over who had the right to be represented at a pub called the Fox and Goose.

When the conference got round to Grunwick on the Tuesday of the conference, it was a foregone conclusion that there would be a lot of bluster about bringing the company to its knees. True to form, the delegates voted for a resolution calling for increased pressure on Grunwick, a trade blockade and so on. Newspaper headlines proclaimed that the TUC had declared war on Grunwick. Yet significantly the debate was brief, and many of the union leaders seemed to have little stomach for it. Apart from anything else, the effort to put the squeeze on Grunwick had made them uneasy allies of the Socialist Workers' Party and the Right to Work Movement (no relation to the American group of the same name, which opposes compulsory unionisation) who had been jostling TUC delegates and spitting at Joe Gormley, the miners' president. For another, the mood was obviously beginning to spread that Grunwick might be more than an embarrassment to the TUC; it could be a humiliation, if all the pressure brought to bear failed to make the company submit. Trade union leaders, like politicians, tend to know a bandwagon when they see one. An increasing number had apparently begun to believe that the wisest course would be to discreetly resign themselves to the fact that Grunwick would hold out, and dissociate themselves from future strike action that might leave them with egg on their faces.

True, there was more talk about blacking our vital services—water, gas and electricity. But a man from the Water Board who came to take a discreet look shortly afterwards said to the director who questioned him, 'Don't worry, if they turn off your water, I'll come back here with a police escort and turn it back on'. We had looked into these matters carefully, and we were convinced that—even if the unions carried out their threat of criminal action—the company could still struggle through.

But the battle was continuing on the legal front as well. By the time this book appears in print, we will know the decision of the Law Lords on the ACAS appeal on Lord Denning's decision that its recommendation that Grunwick should recognise APEX is null and void. The hearings were scheduled to begin early in November. The company has always said that it will respect the law. There is no law in England that could compel it to reinstate the strikers. It remained to be seen whether some degree of union recognition might be required of it legally against the express wishes of the overwhelming majority of its workforce.

13

The lessons of Grunwick

I am not a philosopher or a political scientist. I am just a small businessman. But what I have lived through has led me to brood on the reasons why Britain has become a society in which workers as well as managers earn far less than those in other industrialised countries, in which people's lives are diminished by the lack of choice, and in which, I believe, there will be few vestiges of freedom left unless the whole trend is reversed.

One symptom of our ills is that it is difficult even to talk about these things in clear and rational terms. We are so hypnotised by the events and ideas of the past that we cannot see the very different shape of our problems today.

For example, I have been described as a 'union-bashing' employer—which is rather like talking about an elephant-bashing terrier. I have been supported by a couple of hundred employees and a few outside friends and against us has been ranged the combined might of the TUC, with over eleven and a half million members, not to mention the government and their other supporters. Yet, as our small band of workers has made its way through a threatening mob thousands strong, that mob has still managed to retain in many people's eyes the image of the suffering underdog bravely standing up to the brutal power of an oppressive feudal society. Anyone who can call himself a unionist can borrow a false moral glamour from the past, even when his actions are in support of a giant establishment and against the freedom of individual workers. For my part I doubt whether the real Tolpuddle Martyrs would have recognised as their rightful descendants the howling crowd of pickets trying by obstruction and threats to prevent some frail girl getting to the job she had made up her mind she wanted to go on doing. Someone once said that we drive forward into the future with our eyes fixed on the rear-view mirror.

I suppose that if any of our politicians and commentators have failed to confront the problem of union power for what it is, the explanation also has something to do with what has been described as 'the inevitability complex'. There has been a widespread assumption since Edward Heath's defeat that no Government in Britain can stand up to the unions, even when they make demands that are felt to be unreasonable by the great majority of electors.

Myself, I refuse to believe that Britain is condemned to live with the kind of overweening trade union power that we have seen exercised in the last few years, and whose full weight has been exerted in an effort to crush Grunwick. If I had thought that, I would have given up the fight long ago and emigrated to Australia to can tropical fruit. (If you have an instinct, after all, there are ways to make a living anywhere where conditions for business still exist.) But I have clung to a belief in the resilience and the capacity for survival of the British people. They have got rid of robber barons in the past. They can do so again. Since Britain virtually invented modern trade unionism, after all, is it not reasonable to hope that Britain might be the place where a civilised solution is found to the problem of combining the trade unions with a healthy economy and a form of society that respects individual freedom?

It was that great Scotsman David Hume who wrote that 'it is seldom that liberty of any kind is lost all at once.' The idea might be put another way. I am told that if you boil a lobster very slowly, gradually increasing the temperature of the water, it will not make a sound, or thrash about, until it is properly cooked. If, on the other hand, you throw the same lobster into a pot of boiling water, it will emit horrific shrieks and thrash about wildly. In Britain, our liberties have been slowly cooked. Yet I have seen heartening signs of a decisive switch in public opinion. According to a Gallup poll published in the *Sunday Telegraph* on 4 September 1977, 75 per cent of those interviewed thought the trade unions had too much power. This included a sizeable proportion of trade union members. Not long before, we had seen the revolt of moderates at British Leyland's Longbridge plant against an effort to stage a disruptive strike. Earlier in the year, we had seen an overwhelming vote amongst IBM's employees against union recognition. Throughout the Grunwick dispute, my own mailbag brought me every day letters of support from all over the country, including letters from trade unionists and even local residents, who might well have blamed us for 'provoking' the mob to walk over their gardens and deafen their ears with their slogans.

I think that these are not isolated symptoms. Britain has never tolerated bullies for long, and the bullying tactics of the trade union bosses over the past few years will surely bring their retribution. I will feel that the stand that we have taken at Grunwick will have been richly rewarded if the country one day produces a government that is prepared to put the unions back in their proper, and rightful place, as representatives of the true interests of their members.

Perhaps the Grunwick conflict, by showing up the unacceptable face of trade unionism, has made this task of reform easier. The trade union movement, through its excesses, and a Labour government which has tolerated them and facilitated them through partisan legislation, have been preparing the ground for a public revolt against union privileges that could make the long needed radical reform of the unions a practical political possibility. It is not for me to suggest everything that might go into such a programme, but I think it should include the following elements:

1 *Limits on picketing* The kind of picketing we have had to endure at Grunwick has nothing to do with persuasion. Indeed, in an age of television and other mass media, it might be argued that there is often no need to picket at all to put your view across. But there is no way that a howling mob of outsiders who have nothing to do with an industrial conflict can be regarded as engaged in the arts of peaceful persuasion. At the very least it should be laid down in law that only workers from a firm that is subject to an industrial dispute

should be allowed to join the picket line. The maximum figure of pickets allowed to stand outside the gates should be severely restricted: six should be a fair maximum, if the aim of picketing really is to persuade.

Without doubt we should resist the union demand that pickets should be allowed to stop vehicles in the street in order to 'persuade' those in them of the justice of their cause. This demand was raised after we started to run the Grunwick bus, on the grounds that the pickets were being prevented from explaining themselves to our workers who were insulated from them inside the bus. But of course it was precisely because the pickets' arguments had for months failed to persuade our workers that the pickets finally took to violent obstruction and obliged us to start running the bus.

2 Tax-free strikes The bulk of union income is tax free because trade unions are classified as provident societies, even though they pay only a derisory proportion of their income in members' benefits. In this respect, they are raising money under false pretences.

Is it really healthy that our trade unions should have such licence to raise huge cash reserves for use as an all-purpose political fund? It is high time for governments in Britain to look at the state of union finances. Union income should be taxed, and proper accounting standards should be demanded of unions just as they are demanded of private corporations.

3 Ban the closed shop The Labour government in Britain has introduced conscription of labour. Britain's iniquitous closed shop law has no parallel in Western Europe and denies the right of the individual not to belong to a union if he does not wish to do so. Unless you are a member of an obscure religious sect, you have no grounds for pleading exemption from the closed shop on moral grounds. This means that the plight of individuals who do not want to join a union for reasons of principle is worse than that of conscientious objectors in wartime; yet can it really be said that the compulsion to recruit people for trade unions is as pressing as the need to recruit soldiers for the nation's defence against a foreign enemy? There can be no comparison between these two utterly different situations. This is why a stronger conscience clause is no answer to the problem of upholding the individual's right not to be coerced into a union against his will. It should in no case be lawful to compel an individual to join a union in order to occupy a certain position. Failing that, individuals should at least be able to claim handsome compensation if they lose their job for refusing to join a trade union.

4 Repeal the Employment Protection Act This act of 1975, like the Closed Shop Legislation of 1974, was part of the price paid by a Labour government for continued trade union support. Our experience with ACAS shows that this body could never claim to be impartial; its statutory duty to extend the process of collective bargaining, as has been seen throughout British industry, is no recipe for industrial peace. If an arbitration service is to play any constructive role in British industrial life, it must be genuinely impartial, and it must not be founded on the assumption that unionisation improves relations between employers and their workforce. In fact, the opposite has nearly always proved to be the case, at least in small businesses where the intervention of a union can destroy the intimate connection between management and staff.

5 Extend democracy inside trade unions The trade unions are not only the most powerful social organisations in Britain; they are also the least democratic. It is wholly unacceptable, especially with the spread of the closed shop, that some unions should be able to finance Communist causes or embark on major strikes without consulting their members, or that union leaders can be elected for life on the votes of only a tiny proportion of the membership. The compulsory introduction of the secret postal ballot would be one method of ensuring a more representative trade union leadership, which should certainly be linked with a rule that all union leaders, like company directors, should submit themselves for re-election at reasonable intervals.

6 Suing for breach of contract The immunity of British trade unions from being sued on civil proceedings is extraordinary. Of course, there is nothing new about it. The problem dates back to the Trade Disputes Act of 1906, introduced by the Liberals in the days when it was possible to believe that if you put a weapon into the hands of the unions, they would never be tempted to use it. But there are no reasonable grounds for supposing that anything is gained by allowing the unions to exercise legal privileges and immunities that do not apply to other sections of society. On the contrary, it is impossible for unionised companies to plan ahead if the union can happily violate any agreement that is entered into. It is also worth noting that unions enjoy other privileges in the course of trade disputes, such as the freedom of union officials to say defamatory things about their employers without being sued for defamation. Surely the principle to be applied is that equality under the law is the basis of Britain's tradition of freedom and civil rights. As Lord Denning said, 'Be you ever so high, the law is above you.'

7 *The guarantee of essential services* It should be clearly unlawful to tamper with services that affect the health and public safety of the community. The effect of the Tories Industrial Relations Act of 1971 was to repeal some earlier legislation outlawing strikes that affected vital services such as gas, water and electricity. What is needed is a new essential services act that would again impose limits to industrial disruption in those areas of industry that affect the safety of all.

I realise that, in the late 1970s and in a state that has become as corporatist as Britain, such proposals would seem very radical—perhaps too radical for many people to accept. I am not a politician, and it is not for me to judge the practicality for turning such proposals into action. But I do feel that, if Grunwick has shown anything, it is that the malady of present day Britain will not be cured until the country has found a solution to the problem of trade union power.

I, for one, have no wish to live or work in a country where the dominant voice is that of trade union officials who were never elected by the people as a whole. If our workers wish to join a union we will not deprive them of that right; but equally, we will not acquiesce in the schemes of those who seek to deprive them of the right not to join a union against their wishes.

Power is what is at stake, but there is much more involved than power. I agree with the revolutionaries in one thing: Britain is caught up in an ideological struggle, a conflict that presents a choice between two fundamentally different forms of society. One is the big brother society, where the state and the union bosses control everything, and people are not free to choose their own lives. I cannot understand how anyone could wish to live in this kind of society, but I suppose that there is such a thing as the fear of freedom. Maybe there are people who would be happy to live in a sort of battery-hen society, where the agony of having to take decisions for themselves—or of running the risks of taking the reward of their own efforts—would be taken away from them.

But it is the other alternative that seems exciting and creative to me: the creation of a free society in which people have equality of opportunity to get ahead and make a way for themselves in life. In the past, sheer poverty and the survival of oppressive social forms deprived many people of that opportunity. Today the barriers are different. There is still poverty, of course, though far less than at any time in the past; but for most people the great danger lies in the growing assumption that only the big corporation has a future, that the individual must conform to the demands of the organised group.

This is what I fear most of all. I cannot emphasise too strongly that what I oppose is the corporatist mentality itself, whether the people who succumb to it think of themselves as being on the left or the right. I should feel just as strongly about a right-wing move to give monopoly powers and legal immunities to big business as I do about giving those powers and immunities to monopoly unions.

That is why in the end this is a moral issue. Of course the prosperity of Grunwick was also involved. Of course I hoped to run the company in a way that would make it profitable and make it possible to pay better wages to everyone who worked in it. Of course I hoped to take my fair share of that increased prosperity. But if that had been all, if I had been making a simple calculation about the best chances of putting up my own income, I would have been a great fool to undergo everything that has happened over the last year or two rather than concede the limited union entry which is what APEX claims to be its only demand.

It is because so many people have understood that corporatism is a big moral issue that the doings of one small company have assumed so much importance. This book is open-ended in the sense that our story is not finished, and our very survival is by no means guaranteed. But whatever the conclusion of the tale turns out to be, I will never regret the stand we have taken. In the words of the great Frenchman, de Tocqueville, 'I should have loved freedom, I believe, at all times, but in the time in which we live I am ready to worship it.'